Further Country Matters

Further
Country Matters

Duff Hart-Davis

SWAN·HILL
PRESS

Illustrations by Nicholas Hall.

Copyright © 1992 by Duff Hart-Davis

First published in the UK in 1992
by Swan Hill Press
An imprint of Airlife Publishing Ltd

British Library Cataloguing in Publication Data
A catalogue record for this book
is available from the British Library

ISBN 1 85310 323 3

Printed by Livesey Ltd, Shrewsbury

Swan Hill Press
An imprint of Airlife Publishing Ltd
101 Longden Road, Shrewsbury SY3 9EB

Contents

Author's Preface

In the summer of 1986, when the *Independent* was taking shape in the mind of its founder-editor Andreas Whittam Smith, I asked if he was planning to include a country column in his new paper. Finding that he was, I asked him to consider me as a possible author. 'What sort of a column would you write?' he asked, and I had to confess that I was not sure, as I had never tried to produce one before. I had lived all my life in the country, but had always found editorial executives little interested in what went on outside the cities in which most of them lived.

Happily, after a couple of trial runs, I became the author of the new *Independent*'s Country Matters column when the paper was launched in October 1986. After a long spell of appearing at the foot of the leader page every Saturday, the column was moved into the second half of the paper, and many readers, not finding it, concluded that it had been suppressed. But it was still very much alive, and later it went back to its original position, where it has remained ever since.

One earlier selection of articles was published in book form during 1988. The present harvest is culled from the period March 1988 to March 1992. Readers will scarcely need reminding that the aim of the column has always been extremely modest. It does not seek to maintain a frenzied topicality, to explain the latest technicalities of EEC legislation, or to influence Governments on future agricultural policy. Its aim is merely to share the enjoyment which I derive from living in the country, to record events both ridiculous and sombre, and to capture some of the rustic characters who enliven our green and pleasant land.

January

Dawn on the Downs

For a racehorse in training, the last day of one year is no different from the first of the next: even in the depths of winter the age-old routine of early-morning exercise rolls on remorselessly, and to the pampered creatures in the stables the only change is that on 1 January they all, without knowing it, officially become one year older, no matter their actual date of birth.

So it was that as we drove up the Lambourn Valley in Berkshire before dawn on Tuesday, the last day of 1991, the only lights showing in the blackness were those of racing stables already on the go. My driver and guide was Lady Eliza Nugent, who owns the Mandown Gallops on the downs above Upper Lambourn and manages them for the benefit of the whole equine community.

On our way up the valley she told me a little local history. The Nugent family has been prey to the racing bug for generations: it was her father-in-law Sir Hugh Nugent who laid out the gallops in the 1930s, but the mania had set in long before his day. Hugh's grandfather, Sir Charles, was a compulsive gambler and would bet on which of two flies climbing a wall would reach the ceiling first. The result was that when his son broke his neck and was killed riding in a race at Ostend in his twenties, the family was left with very little money.

Thus Hugh was brought up by his grandfather in penury; but family fortunes revived in 1927 when the old man died and Hugh's grandmother married E.J. King, the shipping magnate. By then Hugh had been fired with a vision of making Lambourn a great training centre, and on land given by his step-grandfather he laid out the gallops — one of them, it is said, by riding a motor-cycle in a circle, holding the outer end of a string attached to a post in the centre.

His main assets were the huge open spaces of the downs, with their natural chalk drainage and their matchless turf, much of which had never been ploughed. Intelligent management of those assets has indeed turned Lambourn into a national training centre, second only to Newmarket in terms of flat racing, and unequalled when it comes to jumping (for Newmarket has no fences).

Over the past twenty years the centre of operations has shifted up the valley. Commuters working in such places as Swindon, Reading and London Airport have invaded Lambourn proper, and the consequent increase in traffic has made the roads dangerous for horses, especially at daybreak. Most trainers have therefore settled in Upper Lambourn, immediately below the main gallops.

Today nearly 1,000 horses are in training there, and teenage boys flock to work as stable lads from far and wide, not least from Ireland, betting and drinking their wages away as lads have for generations. The entire economy of the village depends on racing.

At Eliza's own little yard, Limes Farm, we found her horses still comfortably ensconced on beds of shredded newspaper — a salutary warning for journalists — but ready to set out as soon as the light was strong enough. Normally she would have transferred to the old racehorse on which she rides out, partly to keep an eye on her own pupils, partly to do what she calls 'a bit of policing'. On Tuesday, however, she stayed in the Land Rover for my benefit and drove on up to the Downs.

Seven hundred feet above sea-level, the scene was magical. Partridges called in the half-light. Intermittent drizzle swept from the south-west, and everywhere, going in all directions, were ghostly, shadowy, dark horses: horses walking, trotting, cantering, galloping, horses heard but invisible, horses passing heraldically in lines of distant black silhouettes against the dawn sky.

As we stood near the end of one of the all-weather tracks — a bed of wood shavings laid over gravel — they started pounding uphill from our left. To begin with, the first indication of every new arrival was the taut, rhythmic snorting of an animal reined in to a canter; then, as the light grew stronger, we could see them coming in an endless stream, with their lads (or lasses) standing high in their stirrups as they applied the brakes. Eliza explained that although there is no written rota or timetable, different stables have slightly different routines, so that the strings slot in one after another without having to wait.

It was extraordinary to reflect that the cumulative value of these horses must run to several million pounds. None, probably, was worth less that £5,000; some would fetch over £100,000. Every one was costing at least £10,000 a year to train. Some had won races already, and others would do so; but many would never progress as far as the starting-post.

Trainers prefer their horses to take fast exercise on turf, and normally, by Christmas, the gallops are starting to get cut up; in the past few years, however, the climate seems to have changed for the drier, and this winter the ground is so hard that more and more horses are sticking to the softer all-weather tracks.

One result is that the turf itself looks wonderful. Full daylight revealed it in all its glory: an extraordinary mat of silken fescue grass, six inches long, as thick and resilient as a cushion.

Woe betide the ignoramus who drives a vehicle on to this hallowed carpet. This, or any lesser felony, will immediately bring down the wrath of Eddie Fisher, Head Gallop Man, who has worked here for the past thirty-six years. Tall and lean, with a magnificently weather-beaten complexion, Eddie bounds about his 500-acre kingdom at the speed of a Derby-winner, brandishing the long-handled fork with which he raises divots.

He it is who keeps the turf in its perfect state. In summer the grass is topped every few days, but never cut to a length of less than six inches, and hardly ever rolled. Excessive rolling, says Eddie, makes the ground like a pudding: 'Then it's, *plom, plom, plom,* like on a racecourse,' he says. 'You can hear 'em plutting through it.' Rather than create such a morass, he and his assistants are constantly lifting and patting with their forks.

On Tuesday we found Eddie racing about the Schooling Area, where jumpers are put through their paces over lines of fences. We had hoped to see one of Lambourn's rising stars, Party Politics, who is trained by Nick Gaselee, being schooled by Richard Dunwoody, but somehow we missed him.*

As luck would have it, we were also denied one of Lambourn's most celebrated sounds — that of the trainer Jenny Pitman roaring obscenities such as few men would dare to utter. In the reverent words of one local, 'She don't 'alf turn the air blue some mornings'.

That morning, the air over the Downs remained pearly grey; but I had the compensation of gazing into the wonderful natural amphitheatre of Mandown Bottom, where Hugh Nugent laid out his circular gallop sixty years ago. No wonder horses, like humans, find exhilaration in such elemental surroundings: any sentient creature must surely respond to these high and open spaces, as wild and empty as they were in neolithic times.

Back in the village, as nine people with glowing faces sat down to mountains of eggs and bacon in the Gaselees' farmhouse kitchen, I felt I had caught a glimpse of a ritual as mysterious and archaic as any practised on those downs since the dawn of history.

* Party Politics won the 1992
Grand National.

How White was Our Valley

Meteorologically speaking, last Sunday was the most fascinating day I can remember.

We woke at seven to find ourselves in the middle of another blizzard, with the temperature six degrees below zero; and our first task — as always in the depths of winter — was to feed and water the animals. Since all outside pipes had long since been frozen, there was nothing for it but to carry out buckets of hot water.

Trudging uphill with a 25lb burden in either hand is no joke in any weather, but at least it is easier in fresh, deep snow than on ice. That morning the snow was perfect powder, so light that it rose in clouds from every footfall — the kind that Alpine resorts pray for.

The trick with water-troughs in severe weather — we had discovered over the past few days — is not to fill them to the top; if you do that, you are confronted in the morning with ice solid to the lip, and hot water poured on top simply runs away over the edge. Better to leave the level lower, and fill moderately on top of it. Such had been the frost that several troughs had frozen from the sides and bottom as well as from the top; and I found that, when all else failed, a heavy-headed Canadian axe, designed for splitting wood, was the best weapon for hacking into the ice.

By the time I took the dogs out, after breakfast, the blizzard had abated, but the sky was still heavy and the light thick. No human or vehicle had been up our lane, and even the tell-tale tracks of a fox — single footmarks set out elegantly in a straight line — had been almost obliterated during the past hour or so. I reflected on how much more difficult things would have been if a gale had accompanied the snow; as it was, we had had almost no wind, and minimal drifting. One good blow, and the lane would have been shoulder- instead of shin-deep.

Up in the wood, an immense and sinister silence prevailed. No bird called, no animal moved. My footsteps caused not the slightest sound: the snow did not even creak under my weight. It was as if the eight-inch white blanket had snuffed out all life. Designers of Christmas cards would have felt embarrassed to have created a scene of such extravagance: every twig and branch so loaded that visibility was reduced to a few yards.

At least, I thought, this snow is what foresters have been craving — for when it melts, the water will seep slowly into the ground and filter down to replenish subterranean aquifers, rather than running off uselessly into streams, as heavy rain is inclined to do.

Even if eight inches of snow equal only one of rain, that will still be a help for, as we all know, one inch of rain is the equivalent of 22,000 gallons per acre, and that amount, applied slowly, will do its bit towards quenching the land's thirst.

On top of the hill, snowfields stretched trackless and immaculate to the horizon, but in the dead, white light humps and hollows blended imperceptibly into one another, making progress difficult. The labradors became little black snowploughs, chesting channels through the powder; whenever, at intervals, they reported back for a conference, they looked like ancient sea-lions, since they sported heavy white beards, and their whiskers were bejewelled with crystals of ice.

High over the valley three buzzards came wheeling, and their piercing whistles seemed to rebound from the frozen land. What they were calling about, I could not tell, but it struck me that raptors must do well in such weather, for rabbits, rats and mice show up far more boldly than usual when they move on a white background; and a carpet of snow, reflecting light back into the sky, has the effect of advancing dawn and retarding dusk, so that it increases the time during which hawks can hunt.

As we floundered towards the head of the stream, the sun came labouring over the eastern skyline, veiled in a thick haze — not red or white or yellow, but an extraordinary salmon pink, the kind of colour the Ancient Mariner might have described. It made me think of the three ghostly suns at which the wanderer gazes in Schubert's *Winterreise* — but this was only one, and in any case it was soon gone. For a few minutes it climbed from the horizon like an immense hot-air balloon; then slowly the haze enfolded it, and the sky went grey-white once more.

Seen from above in distant prospect, our valley looked bleak and unfamiliar, distorted by the prominence of walls and hedges, which stood out black and angular between expanses of white. At home, the cats were taking heavy toll of birds made weak and slow by the cold. The bay tree outside the back door proved particularly dangerous territory: being thick and bushy, it offered good shelter, yet as I looked out of the window I saw one of the cats suddenly launch herself through it and crash out the other side with a wren in her jaws. When I tried to snowball the cat, to make it drop the bird, I found that the snow was so powdery that it would not bind at all.

By mid-morning our top field was entertaining a dozen tobogganers of all shapes and sizes, some of them so agile that they could come down the steep slope standing up on their sledges. Others used nothing more sophisticated than fertiliser sacks, but they too went like rockets, and had to fling themselves off before they hurtled into the fence half way down the hill.

Watching them, I felt torn between conflicting inclinations. One was to charge them rent for the use of the slope; the other, more philanthropic, was to go out and dismantle a stretch of the fence, so that they could extend their runs for another 150 yards. In the end I did nothing — except to decide that, the weather being what it was, I should tincture my coffee with rum.

After lunch, a change stole into the valley, visually imperceptible, but obvious to face and hands: for the first time in ten days the breeze went into the west, the air softened, the temperature rose to freezing-point, and the texture of the snow changed. From being uncompactible, it suddenly became ideal for snowballs and snowmen.

After nights at minus ten, and days at minus five, zero felt positively tropical, and at evensong in the village church (congregation four) the temperature indoors was markedly lower than that outdoors, even though the heating had been on for some time. As the rector had, quite rightly, ordered our eighty-year-old organist to stay at home, we had to do our best with the hymns unaccompanied, breath smoking in the air.

Back at the farm, I tackled a task which had been on my mind for days: the construction of an extra skin of plywood for one of the beehives, to give better insulation. The job proved easier than I had expected, and I soon had an outer shell in position; but whether or not it will save the colony inside, only time will show.

Towards sunset, as we were once again feeding and watering, the western sky began to clear. The heavy grey clouds at last broke up, and through them came a blast of low sunlight, which turned the snow pink and lit up every footprint, every sledge-track, every bump and hollow in soft relief. Glorious as it seemed, that dying glow proved cruelly deceptive, for the feeling of warmth which it gave was false. Even as it faded, the temperature was diving through zero again, and every creature living in the open faced another bitter night.

An Elephant for the Garden

So far as I know, there is only one African elephant under construction in Gloucestershire at the moment, but he is going to be — already is — an absolute cracker. His plaster model stands nearly twelve feet high, weighs three tons, and has tremendous presence: cast in bronze, it will no doubt be even more commanding.

When the thirty-six-year-old sculptor David Lomax was asked to take on the assignment, he hardly knew whether or not the proposal was serious. As he says, if the call had come from anyone except John Aspinall, zoo-proprietor extraordinary, he would have dismissed it as a joke.

But Aspinall was in earnest. Last February, in the 'Heroes and Villains' column of the *Independent* Magazine, he chose as his idol 'the desert elephant known to everyone in the Kaokoveld of northern Namibia as the Hoarusib bull', and described what an impression this tremendous animal had made on him when he saw it a year earlier.

Master of a dwindling herd, the bull is about forty-five years old, and seems to have almost supernatural powers in the matter of evading poachers. He also assumes a closely protective role, unusual in an adult male, when young animals are orphaned, and in general is credited with exceptional sagacity.

It remains to be seen whether or not he can save his kind from extinction: the population of desert elephants in Namibia has fallen from 1,000 at the turn of the century to only about seventy, and their chances of survival are slim. More nomadic than their cousins in lusher parts of Africa, they feed up and down the dry river-beds which run out to the Skeleton Coast, and cover as much as thirty miles a day in search of water; but, as in other areas, their range is shrinking and they are threatened not only by poachers, but by the herdsmen and farmers whose land they share.

Aspinall's friends say that he identifies personally with the Hoarusib bull, and that in this mighty animal he discerns a reflection of himself, the last great patriarch of his tribe. Whatever the truth of that, he also sees the animal as a powerfully emotive symbol of the species' fight for survival, and it was partly in order to create publicity for the elephants' plight that he conceived the idea of a statue.

Claiming that he himself could not afford the outlay — over £70,000 — he persuaded his friend the Iraqi-born millionaire Selim Zilkha to commission the sculpture. Mr Zilkha, founder of Mothercare and numerous other enterprises, now lives in Los Angeles, and it is there, outside his house at 750 Lausanne Road, that the great bronze beast is destined to stand.

The creation of it has proved no mean undertaking. David Lomax has made other animals, but never a life-sized pachyderm, and was understandably nervous about the sheer size of the task: thinking about how to tackle the job was almost worse than the work itself, and in all the project will occupy a year of his time.

For a start, the statue is not just a representation of any old elephant, but a portrait, faithfully taken from photographs and from life. To size up his subject, Mr Lomax spent a fortnight in Namibia, tracking the bull with the help of local guides. He was greatly taken with the elephants, and in particular by the lightness of their movement — especially when, one morning, tracks showed that several had passed within five yards of his tent during the night without him hearing a sound.

'They're such massive creatures,' he says, 'and yet they move like the wind. They aren't like horses, which smack their feet into the ground: they seem to float. When I saw them in the distance with their legs hidden by grass, they reminded me of old-fashioned sailing ships, cruising along, with their ears flapping like sails.'

Mr Lomax normally works in a studio at Swindon. For this jumbo operation, however, he needed a foundry with 'really serious lifting gear', and after inspecting several possible workshops he settled on the Pangolin Editions foundry at Chalford, near Stroud, which has a strong tradition of producing sculpted animals — latest and by no means least Philip Blacker's bronze of Desert Orchid, now at Kempton Park.

I found the elephant-builder covered in white dust and perched on a small scaffold, half way up the flank of his model, carving creases into its plaster skin with chisel, adze, knives and a variety of home-made scrapers. Against a fearful jangle of hammering, banging and clashing from other parts of the foundry, to say nothing of screeching pop music, he explained that he had started with a maquette only a few inches high, progressed to a quarter-scale model, and then, by using a grid-pattern, expanded the proportions to life size.

The skeleton of his monster is a framework of steel tubes welded together, its skin a coat of plaster four inches thick, its ears great sheets of resin. Even in its unfinished state, the elephant is an extraordinary sight, breathtaking in its size and presence. To suggest the lightness which so captivated him in the desert, Mr Lomax has set its right forefoot in a lifted position, with the toes just touching the ground.

Apart from that, he has 'tried to go for a very still composition', and to suggest the bull's composure by accentuating the weight-taking, architectural principles — very similar to those of a building — on which an elephant is constructed. 'It wasn't as if the animal had to show off,' he recalls. 'He was so much in charge that he had a kind of restrained power. Big and impressive as he was, I saw a quality of gentleness about his eye.'

All this — it seems to me — Mr Lomax has caught miraculously. He is still a bit worried about the forehead, which strikes him as looking too heavy, but he will soon have that excavated into shape.

Loops of wire protruding through the flanks of the plaster skin show where the model will be cut into pieces for casting, which is due to start next month. The first big section will be the head, minus ears and trunk, and part of the shoulder; the second will be the rib-cage, the third the hindquarters. Tail, legs, trunk and ears will all be cast separately, and there will be ten moulds in all.

The sheets of bronze, a quarter of an inch thick, will then be welded together. The welds will be chiselled off, smoothed over and textured, and the entire statue, weighing four tons, will be given a matt finish like that of the skin of the live animal.

The shipping of it to Los Angeles in a purpose-built crate, sometime towards the end of this year, promises to be an event in itself. As the sculptor remarks, 'it would be easier to shift a Challenger tank'.

The question remains as to what should happen to the plaster model. Normally, after casting, the pieces lie about mouldering on the floor of the foundry — and indeed Desert Orchid, plastered and legless, is lying in just such a fashion at the moment.

The model of the Hoarusib bull is so splendid in itself that it should surely survive. Maybe, if it could be weatherproofed, it might find a home in the garden of the excellent Nature in Art gallery near Gloucester. Meanwhile, only time will show what effect the notorious smogs of Los Angeles have on corrugated bronze skin: perhaps in a few years Mr Zilkha will be the proud possessor of the greenest elephant in the world.

Dark Winter Days

You might not think that the exhumation of a parsnip could become a traumatic event — but then you do not know our parsnips or the depth of the soil in my vegetable garden. From the width of its shoulders, I could see that this particular specimen was a monster, and I approached it with all due reverence, not trying to dig it up in one movement, but first excavating earth all round it to give better access to its lower reaches. Only when its top ten inches or so were standing clear did I drive my spade down into the bowels of the earth where I judged its root must be.

Then, grasping it and pulling upwards with my left hand, and levering on the spade with my right, I began to exert pressure. When nothing happened, I pushed and pulled harder. . . until suddenly, with a sharp crack, the handle of my favourite, unbreakable, stainless steel spade came clean in half.

The implement had long outlived any guarantee which it might once have carried: besides, its markings had been rubbed off, so that I could not even tell what make it was, and therefore had no hope of gaining redress from the manufacturers. As I surveyed the jagged, broken ends, I reluctantly came to the conclusion that, by the time the parsnip reached our plates, this one vegetable would have cost at least £60.

The setback led me to reflect on the satisfaction gained now, at the dead of winter, from using produce grown, harvested or stored when summer was at its height. Obviously no parsnip is worth £60 — but who can put a price on the pleasure of having one's own honey, glowing golden in jars on the larder shelf? Who can say what it is worth, while freezing fog blankets the valley, to have one's mind transported back to the heat of July and August by that enticing sight?

For some reason last year's honey ripened to exactly the right consistency. In my experience, all honey gradually sets and hardens, sometimes to the point at which only a knife will penetrate it: to make it soft again you must cream it, heating it gently and then giving it a stir. The crop of '91, however, has brought itself to an ideal state, easily spooned and spread, but thick enough not to run, so that very considerable amounts can safely be heaped on a spoon or a piece of bread.

Eating it gratefully, I think of the balmy autumn days when I took it: a pre-emptive invasion of the hives one morning, to seal off the upper from the lower racks, and then the final swoop, on a warm, still evening, to remove the honey-laden combs. Both times I was pursued all the way back to the house by a cloud of angry bees from the most militant of my four colonies, but thanks to the efficiency of my protective armour, I escaped without being seriously stung.

Now — I hope — the bees are safely hibernating, each colony packed in a single cluster for warmth, with those on the inside dutifully burrowing outwards every now and then to take over from their colleagues the duty of manning the cold surface stations. In bitter weather such as we have been having, I always fear that a colony may freeze to death; but in fact the bees usually come through, by this process of continuous rotation, and a greater danger than frost is a warm, wet spell, which may encourage them to expend energy by sallying forth and flying about when there is no food to be found.

It is not only humans who benefit from frugal activity undertaken in summer. For the past few weeks our bullocks have been eating the hay which I and my wife made at the end of a fine spell in July. Normally we buy hay, for we do not have enough level land on which to make a worthwhile crop of our own; but last year, in a fit of enthusiasm, we turned ourselves into medieval peasants and built a small rick by hand.

A run of very hot weather was coming to an end. Rain was advancing on us from the Atlantic, and its arrival had been forecast with precision. It seemed a pity to waste the grass which I had cut a few days before in a strip along the lower edge of our top field. I therefore turned the rows a couple of times with the tractor, and on the last afternoon before the storm we set out with forks to collect the dry grass into a heap.

The area was too small for it to be worth our calling in a baler — and in any case, every baler in the district was going all-out before the weather broke. We therefore worked by hand, and found progress disconcertingly slow.

The hay was soft and slippery, so that no great amount could be impaled on a fork at any one stab, and we spent most of the time trudging back and forth between the heap and the ends of the fluffed-up rows, with the distance to be covered constantly increasing. After a while I began to think that some ultra-modern contrivance like a wheelbarrow might speed things up — only to decide that by the time I had loaded and unloaded it at the end of each short traverse, very little would be gained.

And so we laboured on, back and forth, feeling like figures in some old oil painting, and reflecting on how infinitely laborious life must have been in the Middle Ages. Slowly the sun wheeled into the west; the sky was still clear, but a smell of rain stole into the evening air. Although dusk fell with our task unfinished, we had by then built quite a respectable stack, some twelve feet square and eight feet high, and we hastily covered it with polythene sheets against the coming downpour.

The rain arrived soon after dark, but it did no harm to our precious creation, and we later battened the stack down properly to protect it from autumn gales. Over the next few weeks it sank and sank as the hay compacted, until it was scarcely half its former height, and the net result of our labours looked ridiculously small.

Then, in mid-winter, came the moment of truth. Would the cattle eat it? To us, the hay neither looked nor smelled very nice: it had a rather dowdy, dull appearance, and lacked the delicious aroma of freshly-baked biscuits which clings to hay made quickly and stored at exactly the right moment.

Imagine our relief, then, when we opened the stack and the bullocks went for it with relish, eating it in preference to some professionally-made hay which we had bought in. As with the parsnip, the intrinsic value of the crop is insignificant, and yet the sight of the cattle munching it in the frost brings back to life that glorious summer day when we toiled like slaves beneath a burning sun.

Contemplation of ash-logs, burning with a bright flame, induces similar memories — although these are not of last summer, but of the one before. Although I cannot usually recognise individual pieces of wood, I can determine their provenance from their position in the stack, and so remember where I cut them. Now, gazing into the fire on an icy evening, I see a windblown trunk lying on top of a badger sett, and hear woodpigeons cooing lazily. Like the hay, each log is worth far more for its associations than for its calorific value.

I do not know if the squirrel, now snugly tucked up in his drey with his tail curled over his head, dreams of summer as I do. All I can say for sure is that I derive a good deal of harmless pleasure from giving rein to the instinct which I share with him, for hoarding nature's bounty against the dark days of winter.

Avebury Revealed

Washed by pale winter sunlight, and bedded in smooth-cropped turf, the sarsen stones of Avebury were looking their most magnificent and timeless. Yet it was not on them but on their lost companions that our attention was focused.

As my friend advanced over the grass, the forked stick in his hands suddenly lifted, 'Up!' he called, 'two . . . three . . . four . . . down.' Moving away to one side, he made another inward pass over the same area, and the same thing happened, only this time to a count of six. So precise was the reaction of his stick that he could map out not only the corners of the bed in which a mighty oblong stone had lain, but also traces of the scallops and indentations along its sides.

Ted Fawcett has been able to dowse all his life: when he was thirteen, he saw a group of people standing on the lawn at a hotel where his family was staying, went out, was handed a forked stick, and promptly found a blocked drain which had eluded everyone else.

Now in his sixties, and retired after sixteen years as director of public affairs for the National Trust, he is still active as a gardening historian and antiquarian; but recently he has become more and more fascinated by the great stone rings at Avebury and the other prehistoric monuments in the Wiltshire downland around them.

His discoveries — if they are correct — will revolutionise previous theories about Avebury, for they show that the ancient shrine was at least three times as big as any other modern researcher has yet suspected. His extraordinary secret is that he can dowse not merely buried stones, but the sites on which other stones stood or lay before they were broken up and carted off for building in the eighteenth and nineteenth centuries.

After intensive study of dowsing, he concludes that the human body is an extremely sensitive magnetometer, and that the process of dowsing appears to be the reaction of a human being to changes in the earth's magnetic field. Sensors in the soles of the feet, the heels, behind the knees and elsewhere all seem to be part of the body's unconscious balance system, and send signals to the cerebellum, the part of the brain which governs breathing, heart rate, balance and so on.

Mr Fawcett feels that dowsing is a simple, natural activity akin to walking. 'As soon as you start concentrating on how to walk — rise on ball of toe, push off, bring up other foot — you cease to be able to do it, and begin staggering about. You destroy the automatic process that's been working for you.'

Dowsing is the same. Left to themselves, the body's sensors react when their owner passes over a change in the earth's magnetic field, and if he or she is holding an instrument such as a forked stick, L-shaped rods or a pendulum, the reaction is transmitted to it by involuntary movements of the forearms and wrists.

The composition of the instrument is of no importance — wood, metal, whalebone, almost anything will do. It is not the forked stick or angled rod which reacts to stimuli from the earth: it is the body, which transmits them to the instrument.

Yet even Mr Fawcett cannot fully explain what is happening when his stick jumps over the turf at Avebury. What *seems* to be happening is that he is detecting magnetic traces left in the ground by the stones which once lay there.

Avebury is thought to have been built around 2500 BC and used as a shrine for 1,000 years. Even if many of its standing stones then fell down, they must have remained where they were for another 3,000 years at least. Mr Fawcett's theory is thus that after 4,000 years *in situ* each stone has left a magnetic trace in the ground, and this is what he is picking up.

That he *does* pick something up is beyond doubt. Again and again, as I watched, his forked stick jumped vigorously over open ground, and although I could get no reaction from it on my own, when I held one end in my left hand while he held the other in his right, I felt it leap like a jack-in-the-box.

What he has found, in a nutshell, is that at Avebury — as at all other neolithic monuments throughout Europe — the magic number was three. Today only single megaliths mark out parts of the two concentric rings remaining. Mr Fawcett has found not just that there were three enormous rings, rather than two (the one outside the vallum, or rampart and ditch, has gone entirely), but that each of the rings was in triplicate: where every big stone now stands, there were two more whose resting places he can identify with precision.

Besides being vast in extent, the shrine was exceedingly complex. It was approached by avenues of stones, again set out in threes. ('Always in threes,' murmurs Mr Fawcett hypnotically as he sketches a plan, 'always, always.') As the avenues meet the outer circle, at entrances north and south, the stones become smaller, but they march on in threes towards the centre — and there in the middle lies a circular area whose significance had never been understood.

Until now archaeologists have generally called it a blind spring — a spring with no outflow; but to Mr Fawcett it is something quite different. Because he gets a dowsing signal from it, whichever way he approaches, he surmises that it was a ritual area with an artificially hardened floor, perhaps of chalk rammed down and dosed with milk to form a kind of mortar.

One of the most fascinating things about his discoveries is that they fit every known neolithic site in Europe. From the Ring of Brogar in Orkney to Callanish in Lewis, to the Quiberon peninsula in Brittany, our primitive forebears built their shrines in astonishingly similar patterns. Not only that: the settlements in which they lived were all identical. At each of the ritual sites — and in quite unexpected places, such as Osterley Park — Mr Fawcett has detected the remains of dwellings laid out row after row in absolutely precise grid patterns by Stone-Age town planners of unswerving accuracy.

The lot of a dowser is not an easy one. As Mr Fawcett mildly remarks: 'Any reaction from an instrument is believed at once, but one from a human body is immediately discredited.' Moreover, even believers are racked by inexplicable conundrums — among them the fact that magnetic traces of the ritual areas at

Avebury seem to shift a few feet according to the temperature of the air and ground.

Mr Fawcett is puzzled by this phenomenon but not dismayed, for he attributes it to changes in conductivity, and in any case has met it elsewhere. Dowsing for traces of the garden made for Lucy Harrington, Countess of Bedford, between 1617 and 1627 at Moor Park in Hertfordshire, he found a grotto which refused to stay in the same place. Its layout, with steps encircling it on either side, was always the same — but the whole thing could move as much as ten feet depending on moisture and soil temperature. This was, as he remarked, most disturbing.

To a casual onlooker, his work at Avebury is exactly that. No matter that he considers dowsing 'an ordinary reaction of a human body to its environment'. I could not escape the feeling that, if he was not exactly in touch with earth spirits, he was at least making contact with something which had happened an unimaginably long time ago.

February

In the Jaws of Fiery Lane

As soon as the man appeared at our door, I could tell from the look on his face that he was in trouble. Short, middle-aged, balding and clad in a blue overall, he was a truck-driver, if ever I saw one. Before he had spoken a word, I knew that our lane had claimed another victim. Sure enough, he was stuck at the point where the hill starts to become serious, 100 yards above our house, with a load of seed potatoes on board. On his way from Edinburgh to the south west, he had already called at Evesham, and now was trying to make a delivery to our farmer-neighbour, Francis.

He had committed two serious mistakes. The first was to ignore Francis's instructions, given over his radio telephone a few minutes earlier, about the final stages of his route. Do NOT turn right for the village at a certain crossroads, he had been told: carry straight on.

Lured by the name on the signpost, he turned right. At the bottom of a steep, twisting hill he came to the village green. There he made his second error. This time, instead of ignoring advice, he followed it. 'Can I get through there all right?' he asked a woman outside the pub, pointing down the funnel (and in some places more or less tunnel) known as Fiery Lane. 'Oh yes,' she said nonchalantly. 'You won't have any bother.'

With a fifty-four-foot articulated lorry as tall as the roofs of the village houses? With nineteen tons of potatoes on board? She might have been joking — but no; as it was only 10 am, I think she was still half awake.

What the driver could not know was that as soon as he committed himself to the jaws of Fiery Lane, he was as good as doomed. In all its length — about a mile and a half — there was only one spot at which he had any chance of turning. I imagine his heart sank when he reached the lowest point of the road, below the church, and saw the sign saying 'Steep hill 1 in 4.' Yet he had no option but to continue.

He made another 300 yards before his leviathan juddered to a halt, tyres smoking. By then his radio-phone had been put out of commission by the high sides of the valley, and he walked back down to us for assistance. 'It's like the wall of death!' he complained in his Scots accent. 'I've bust one mirror already.'

'You wait,' I told him. 'You're not on the real hill yet.'

I rang Francis, who brought his biggest four-wheel tractor to the rescue. Backing down, he hitched a steel hawser to the front of the truck and began to tow; but the lorry was *so* huge that the tractor looked like a Dinky toy in front of it, and its chances of climbing the hill seemed infinitesimal.

It did not even reach the steep part of the slope. After less than 100 yards, the combination scorched to a halt. A second tractor, hitched to the front of the first, made little difference. The trouble lay mainly in the truck's great length and weight, but also in its width: its wheels were so wide apart that they chewed off the bottoms of the banks on either side and spread a slippery paste of mud and leaf-mould all over the tarmac.

Soon it became clear that the driver's only hope was to back down to the lay-by below the church; and it was not until he began trying to reverse past my own territory that I fully took in the dimensions of his vehicle. On a motorway you would hardly notice it — except that you might be glad to overtake it safely. Here, it was utterly out of place, a monster which actively threatened the environment.

After every few yards its back or front would slide against a bank and become wedged, so that the tractors had to pull it forward again until it was better aligned. Time after time it roared and ground a few yards uphill before beginning to roll back.

It was at this stage that Shalimar, our peacock, decided that enough was enough. Taking the commotion as an insult — a challenge on his own territory — he began to answer every noise with a deafening screech. What with the stricken monster roaring, men shouting and the peacock screaming, we might have been in some hideous urban zoo.

So long as the truck was in the wood, its elephantine side-swipes did not much matter; but when the thing drew alongside our garden, it became a real menace. At one stage the back wheels jammed against the garden wall, which shook as though in an earthquake and threatened to collapse. A few moments later the tailboard fetched up against a building on the other side of the lane.

Next it was within six inches of my study window. Then our telephone line became hooked under the lip of the canopy. Immediately afterwards the cargo of potatoes, bulging through the flexible side-walls, caught on the corner of another building. Some daffodils which had bravely reached a height of four or five inches were mashed to pulp.

Throughout all this the driver remained amazingly calm. He was extremely skilful, and, within the narrow limits open to him, manoeuvred with resource and precision. Many another man would have lost his temper and his head; but only once did this fellow let fly a sudden shout of 'If I ever see that woman again, I'll *shoot* her!' — and even that was uttered in a jocular tone.

His would-be rescuers also remained incredibly good-natured, considering the infuriating nature of their task.

After two hours of all-out struggle, the lorry at last reached the lay-by below the church. Our hope had been that there, on the only wider stretch of road, the tractors would be able to yank it round bodily in its own length, so that it could escape forwards up the slope on the far side.

No such luck. Quickly-taken measurements showed that the length of the vehicle was greater than the width of the road. There was no option for it but to continue backwards.

I myself thought it would never negotiate the steep, uphill bend past the churchyard, and I could not imagine how the saga was going to end. Would the truck have to be unloaded, dismantled and taken away in parts? Would the farmer — a different one, down there — have to bulldoze a special exit into his bottom field?

To cut short another long story, with exemplary patience and ingenuity the extraction team did manage to coax the truck backwards up that awkward pitch, along the level and into a farm track, where — four hours behind schedule — it could at last turn round. A stone wall was (as the local idiom has it) hit down in the process, but no serious damage was done.

Trailing clouds of wrath, Francis bore down on the pub and demanded to see the woman who had dispensed advice so freely, but the landlord declined to produce her. Back at the farm, it was found that the buffeting and shunting had shifted the lorry's cargo, and when the driver unfastened one side-wall, a torrent of potato sacks poured out. These had to be reloaded by hand. Some welding had also to be done, to repair damage to the truck before it went on its way.

Fiery Lane now looks as if Hannibal had used it to train elephants for his passage over the Alps: the banks are ruined, and long stretches of it are knee-deep in mud and smashed branches. Our garden gate will no longer shut.

Clearly, that Scotsman will never attempt it again, but some other visitor may. What we need, as I have said before, is a sign on the village green addressed specifically to the drivers of heavy goods vehicles, with the message: 'Abandon hope, all ye who enter here.'

Apparently in response to this cri de coeur, *the Council did later erect warning notices at either end of the lane.*

Bores of the Year . . .

Not many organisations have the nerve to advertise their own Great Bores of the Year: most would rather keep such monsters under wraps. The National Rivers Authority, however, fearlessly gives advance warning of when its champions are going to perform — and so it was, alerted by an excellent leaflet, *The Severn Bore,* that I found myself drawn to the bank of the river on the tight bend at Stonebench, just south of Gloucester, at 9 am on Thursday.

Several hundred other punters had also heard the call, on a glorious morning of hard frost and hazy sunshine. Wily fanciers parked their cars way back up the lane and walked the last mile or so, and the wiliest of all — your correspondent — took his bike in the back of the car so that he could ride the final stretch.

On the bank of the river there was plenty of room for all. Some fancied the bend itself as a vantage-point; others, myself included, went on along the towpath to a hump which commanded a straight run downstream.

The bore — my leaflet informed me — is the wave which forms when an exceptionally high tide forces its way up the narrowing channel of the Severn. Stonebench is one of the best view-points, because the banks there are steep, and the bore is funnelled into its most impressive form — a wall of water six feet high surging upstream at ten mph.

The NRA rates bores by a system of stars, one (small) to four (large). Thursday's was the only four-star bore predicted for this spring, and the next will not occur until 29 August. It was a rare creature, then, that we were all awaiting. Many of those present had never set eyes on it; others had seen it dozens of times, but still came back. One party of three calculated that, in aggregate, 120 years had gone by since their first and only previous sighting.

According to the timetable given by the NRA, the bore was due to reach us at 9.26 am. People seemed happy to wait, and they all stood gazing in expectation down-river as if they were expecting some messiah to come sweeping up the stream. The sun grew warm on our backs. The meadows slowly changed from white to green as the frost went off the grass. Beneath our feet the great brown river floated on, treacly and silent, with a few pieces of driftwood sailing past to show the speed of the current.

Minutes ticked by. The set time came and went. Who or what had blundered — the river authority or the moon? Those of us with binoculars were watching a man in black on the bank at the end of the straight, half a mile away. He could see round the next bend, and became our marker. For as long as he was walking about, we knew we could relax.

9.36, and still nothing. 9.40. At last we saw him straighten up and level his camera. Somebody shouted, 'It's coming!' — and there it was. Explosions of spray along the banks were the first we saw of it. Then suddenly the great wave itself was in sight, speeding straight towards us.

Three lively motorboats skimmed and bounced ahead of it. Surfboarders in wet-suits rode it until they toppled off. Huge gouts of brownish water leapt from its edges as it thundered into cavities and bays along the banks. Never mind that the thing was twenty minutes behind schedule: here it was — majestic and awe-inspiring. A few people shrieked as spray hit them, but most fell silent, struck dumb by that tremendous, elemental surge of power.

The leading wave was at least six feet high, and behind it came two others. All three were past us in an instant, but behind them the whole river had changed from a mill pond to an angry, seething ocean, and its level had risen ten feet or more.

I cannot believe anyone went away disappointed. The spectacle, though brief, had been thrilling, and I felt thoroughly gruntled as I slipped away a few miles downstream to compare notes with that veteran seafarer, farmer and cider-maker Jasper Ely, who lives right on the bank of the Severn at Framilode.

There the river channel is much wider, and the bore correspondingly less spectacular; but Jasper knows as well as anybody how unpredictable the high tides can be. His house is separated from the river by an earth bank, a lane and a low brick wall, but twice in the past fifteen years he has had water in the house up to the surface of the kitchen table.

Imagine a rubicund face set in a halo of white whiskers, a generous figure and still more generous tattoos. A small round cap, worn indoors as well as out, and an old white sweater complete the image of an ancient mariner. Get Jasper talking about the bore, and your morning is made.

On Thursday, as I arrived, the river opposite his door was brimming, and a few inches of water had run into the lane. But that proved the height of the flood, and no damage was done.

'Trouble is,' said Jasper, 'you can't trust the bugger. A lot of things affect him. If you've got the wind sou'-west, or sou'-sou'-west, it blows him a bloody sight bigger, whereas if the wind's down on him, nor'-nor'-east, it'll cut him, and he won't be so big.

'Of course, to us river folk, there's no such thing as a bore. You use that word: it shows you're a stranger! To us he's the flood head. Now on the Humber, they have a big tide there as well. I seen him once, but he was a poor old thing. Anyway, he's called a 'hygre' — an old English word . . .'

Three years ago Jasper and his farming partner Pete Smythies threw a bore party, inviting patrons from a local hostelry called the Bohemia, and elsewhere, to breakfast. From the nearby village of Uley came Chas Wright, the brewer, bearing barrels of his Old Spot ale. From Jasper's own cider shed came home-made cider and perry. From the farmyard came a young boar, which they barbecued whole in the open.

The guests arrived and parked their expensive cars on the bank. The bore went past. They drank its health, whacked into slices of sizzling pork, and washed them down copiously. But then the river struck back. Forty minutes after the bore had gone by — the moment when the flood-tide peaks — water crept over the grass beside the lane. Let Jasper take up the story.

'Soon as I saw that, I shouted, "Look out — we're going to get a drop! Block the bloody drains!"'

'I *told* they know-all buggers from Bristol to leave their cars up the Darell [the pub], didn't I? "Oh," they said, "he'll never get up here, will he?' Well, as it turned out, he bloody did!'

Jasper waded out to rescue his chickens, and made a fine sight standing thigh-deep in the road with one under each arm. But the car-owners were too late.

'Next thing, we've got a nice shiny white BMW with a briefcase floating round the headrest. A Sierra with water up to the steering wheel. One bloke's got a company car, another his missus's — oh dear!'

Injury was added to insult when some of the birds took refuge on top of the stranded automobiles. As Jasper recalls, 'It was fowl-shit on the roof and flood water inside. They weren't very happy with that.'

No such accidents took place on Thursday, but Jasper remains adamant that it never does to trust the river: 'Down at Sharpness, he nearly always works spot on, but up here there's nothing definite about the bastard, and you'd better bloody watch him . . . '

. . . and Boars for the Table

Once when my brother was teaching as a volunteer in India, he wrote home from Uttar Pradesh to say that someone in the vicinity had shot a wild boar ten feet long. 'Uttar Rubbesh!' replied my father crisply. 'Bores that size occur only in my club, the Garrick.'

The exchange floated through my mind as I leant over the wall of a sty at Fosters Farm, at South Barrow in Somerset, and sized up a Polish wild boar of no mean dimensions. I cannot claim that he was ten feet long, but he was built like a tank, and his owner, Nigel Dauncey, reckoned that he must already weigh about 500lb, even though he is still a youngster.

The most striking fact about him though, was that he was completely tame. He was hirsute and black, and perhaps a shade more highly strung than a domesticated pig, but he engaged in perfectly normal porcine conversation with visiting humans, paid no attention to the farm Rottweiler snuffling about, and, when a cat appeared on the wall, merely raised his nose and gave it a friendly sniff.

It is now six years since Mr Dauncey established the Barrow Boar enterprise on his 350-acre farm, and in that time he has pioneered the commercial production of wild boar in this country. His first four animals came from zoos, and, even though they were surplus to requirements, cost between £800 and £900 apiece. Since then he has blended in stock of German, Danish, French and Polish origin, and has built up to a strength of more than forty breeding sows. He now also runs an advisory service for other farmers planning to go into the business — an expensive move, as a gilt (or young sow) still costs about £650.

His object all along has been to keep the breed as pure as possible, and he considers it an advantage to have started with zoo or park animals, whose blood has not been contaminated by crossing with that of domestic pigs. Some European stock, in contrast, has degenerated through uncontrolled miscegenation: during the second world war many domestic animals escaped or were turned loose and made their way into the forests, where they readily mated with their wild cousins.

In England, *Sus scrofa* survived in the wild until the sixteenth century, having been hunted for centuries by monarchs and prized for the richness and delicacy of its meat. Today, Mr Dauncey's aim is to make that meat widely available again — and to this end, his animals live as natural a life as possible.

They spend most of their time out in fields, where their staple diet is grass. Contrary to popular belief, they do not dig up everything in sight; in fact, during summer, when there is plenty of grass, they hardly dig at all, and they begin serious excavation only in the autumn, when they are looking for roots and grubs. They also get root crops such as sugar beet and potatoes, and in winter their basic ration is organic coarse meal made from germinated wheat, barley, lucerne, beans and molasses, which comes out of the bag moist and smelling delicious.

The fact that they were in farm buildings when I saw them was purely coincidental: in winter they come in for a while, not so much for their own benefit, but more to take the pressure off the land, which happens to be heavy clay. One of their great advantages — to a commercial producer — is that they need so little artificial food, shelter or veterinary care. As long as they have plenty of grass, water, and a good muddy wallow, they are perfectly happy.

Tame as they become with regular handling, they yet retain elements of wildness in their physical make-up. For instance, during the mating season, from November to February, the boars grow huge shields or callouses of skin two inches thick on their shoulders, to protect them from possible assaults by rivals, whose favourite method of attack is to slash backwards with their razor-sharp tusks as they pass.

Once mated, the sows gestate for four months, and then produce an average of five boarlets in each litter. The babies are strongly striped in brown and cream, and look curiously un-pig-like, almost as if they were young deer. When the stripes fade, at about six months, the boar take on the colour of their parents: French strains tend to be pale grey, and are known as silverbacks, whereas Polish boar are red-brown or black.

As with any animal destined for the butcher, it does not do for the farmer to become too fond of any individual. Thus most of the Barrow pigs which go off to the slaughterhouse at the age of twelve or fourteen months have no names. Yet a few leading lights escape this anonymity, and the patriarch of the herd at the moment is Klaus, a fourteen-year-old German boar who was recently modelled by the sculptor Sukie Erland (her original plan was to do some small bronzes, but she was so taken with Klaus that she later conceived the idea of a life-sized replica.)

There is no doubt that boar are making a strong comeback in this country. The Wild Boar Association, founded in 1989, now has a dozen members, and there are several more breeders as yet unregistered. The main worry of the establishment is the import of feral pig meat from Australia, which, though markedly inferior to the real thing, may easily be passed on as wild boar by unscrupulous dealers.

Having mastered the care and breeding of true wild boar, Mr Dauncey is now concerned to expand his market for the meat. At present he himself goes on a delivery run every Tuesday, taking in such far-flung retailers as the Duchess of Devonshire's Chatsworth farm shop, in Derbyshire, and Harrods. He also sells direct to a few high-class restaurants, and in the summer is much in demand to demonstrate his products at agricultural shows.

Prices are high — from the astronomical £13.50 a lb charged by Harrods for loin fillet, down to cubed steak at about £4. But everyone who has tried the meat cracks it up as being something special, so I went in pursuit of some at a splendid outpost of *gourmandise* known as Trencherman's — a kind of miniature Fortnum's, improbably sited next to a butterfly farm in a lovely wooded valley near Sherborne.

There I found that wild boar burgers, introduced last year, have proved a great hit, and that cubed steak has gone down particularly well at events like hunt balls, where some tremendous casseroles have been created. Everyone who tries the meat (I was told) comes back for more. I myself carried off a four-pound joint of leg and a pound of sausages.

With every package comes a sheaf of recipes, most of them rather elaborate, and some positively outlandish ('throw in a few sprigs of fir'). But one fact on which all agree is that wild boar meat should be marinaded before it is cooked — otherwise it may turn out tough.

Our sausages we ate without much ceremony — and extremely good they were, tasty and genuine. The joint we marinaded in red wine for three days, before pot-roasting it. The result was sensational — the most succulent meat that any of us could remember, a kind of big brother to ordinary pork, denser, stronger, more highly flavoured, and reminiscent of venison.

No wonder — we said to ourselves — that wild boar had been the food of kings. But we were luckier than most, in that we were able to wash it down with a right royal beverage — the 1058 O.G. strong ale made by Chas Wright in the village of Uley, and known by the uncommonly apt name of Pigor Mortis.

Heseltine and Hot Air

Over the past few days and nights a notable piece of timber has been slowly going up in smoke. I refer to the section of beech-trunk, about two feet long and eighteen inches thick, into which Michael Heseltine tried to hammer a six-inch nail during the summer of 1977.

Ever since then this hefty lump of wood has played a central part in my existence. Why I originally chose it, I cannot now remember, for in those days we had abundant elm which had died of disease, and elm — as everyone who has struggled with it must know — is even harder, knottier and more impenetrable than beech.

Hardness, knottiness and impenetrability were the qualities I then sought, for at the annual village fete I was undisputed king of the sideshow known as 'Have a Bash', in which contestants were invited to hammer six-inch nails into a baulk of timber. 'Ten pence a nail. Fewest hits wins', said my board. 'Gents' Prize £1 — Ladies' 50p'.

Have a Bash was never a great money-spinner, since it demanded a considerable outlay on nails before any revenue had been taken, and then the accumulation of cash was painfully slow. But it did have the advantage of giving people a chance to let off steam: whereas the tombola and bran-tub treasure-hunt were essentially passive activities, nail-hitting was violent and energetic and good for the release of aggravation.

So there I was, on a fine Saturday in July, with my section of beech-tree, a good supply of nails, and a filthy old metal hammer, rather light, with half its claw missing. I still have the hammer, and I can still hear the despairing cries of 'Bugger!' which the punters uttered as they gave it a practice swing — but I was not going to offer them any better implement. The year before, I had foolishly brought along a hammer with a fine wooden handle, and within quarter of an hour it had been decapitated by people over-reaching in their excitement and hitting the nail with the neck rather than with the head.

Between the coconut shy on one side and bowling for the pig on the other, business proceeded satisfactorily. The log proved exceedingly durable, as I had hoped, with a useful twist in its grain, and hardly anyone was able to drive a nail right home, no matter how many blows he or she might rain on it. Almost all the nails buckled at the third or fourth stroke, bent over, and had to be hammered flat.

After a while the log began to resemble some creature covered in scales or spikes — an armadillo or porcupine — and I kept giving it a bit of a turn so as to present a new face. Wide boys tried to secure permission to hit their nails into one of the sawn ends — down the grain instead of across it; but I was adamant that all entrants had to go in through the bark, from the sides.

Presently along sauntered our local MP, Michael Heseltine, wearing an open-necked Jermyn Street shirt, crisply striped and ironed. Rising to my challenge, he said he would have a go, and to give him a start I set a nail in position with a few little taps. Just as he was squaring up for his first hit, I noticed that a small girl — his daughter — was standing too close for comfort.

'Better move her back,' I said. 'These nails sometimes fly out.'

We manoeuvred the girl out of the way. Heseltine let drive. He missed. He struck again. Once more he missed — though not by much. As hammer smacked into wood, the nail jumped out of its socket and fell over.

'Those two don't count,' I said magnanimously. 'Start again.' I tapped the nail back into position and handed the hammer over.

Once more the fearless Member for Henley and South Oxfordshire let fly. This time he hit, but only just. Suddenly energised by a glancing blow, the nail flew upwards, and its point caught him unerringly in the cleft of the chin. Blood oozed from the puncture and began to drip on his glossy shirt. But the mishap did not deter him, and after a brief pause for mopping-up he tried again.

There is no need for a blow-by-blow description of the farce that followed. Suffice it to say that after twenty-seven hits, and a number of more-or-less legitimate straightenings of the tormented target, the first inch of the nail had gone into the wood and the remaining five were flattened horizontally into the bark.

Mr Heseltine went on his way in good humour, handkerchief to chin. Others came and had a bash. As evening shadows began to fall across the cricket field, the record stood at five for men and eight for women (who were allowed to use five-inch nails). Then along came Ron, a small man, but a professional fencing contractor, who, to the incredulity of the bystanders, sank a six-inch nail to its head with three carefully-measured strokes.

Nobody was going to beat that, so I gave him the £1 prize and prepared to set off for home. Now the question arose: what to do with my bristly monster? I could have cravenly rolled it into the bracken on the common which surrounded the playing field and left it there — but as I myself was in charge of the field, that seemed less than honourable. I therefore, with some difficulty, loaded the log into my trailer and took it home.

For days it lay about in my woodshed with its once-bright nails slowly rusting. It was far too big to go on the fire, yet to have addressed it with a power-saw, full of metal as it was, would have dealt instant death to the chain. Out of interest I weighed it, and found that it turned the scale at just over 200lb, of which perhaps five were steel.

After a while I realised that its role in life must now be that of chopping-block, and on a wet afternoon I devoted an hour to the laborious business of clearing the nails from the sides round one end with hammer and jemmy. That done, it served its new purpose admirably.

March

Dam and Blast!

Anyone whose professional motto is 'Dam and Blast!' must surely be worth a visit — and so it proves with Jack Hatt, veteran farmer and agricultural contractor of Goring Heath, in Oxfordshire. That challenging legend, emblazoned on all his vehicles, signifies that he creates lakes with one hand and blows things up with the other.

If Jack had not existed, H.E. Bates would have had to invent him. With his rubicund complexion, his twinkling eye, his luxuriant side-whiskers (on which a special preservation order has long since been in force), his shatteringly loud tweed suits, and above all his torrent of anecdotes, delivered with terrific relish, he is every inch a pillar of the countryside. Even his limp — the result of a severe motorcycle crash when he was twenty — somehow enhances his stature as a rustic original.

Engage him as the speaker for your cricket or football club dinner, and the evening will be made. But beware: his stories tend to be so fruity that the first two or three may well send the vicar slinking ashen-faced for the exit.

Although born in Essex in 1913, Jack has lived almost all his life where the Chilterns roll down towards the Thames and the Oxford plain. His father, who farmed there, was the last man in the area to use oxen, until about 1920.

Jack himself began agricultural contracting in 1938, when the threat of war produced a tremendous drive to grow more corn. 'I could see this ploughing-up job coming along, so I went and bought a whole lot of big tractors. Then we did PPD and H. That's foxed you, hasn't it? Press, Plough, Drill and Harrow, day and night. Massive great tractor, four-furrow plough, four-furrow press with a seed-box on top of it, half a chain harrow tied on the back — and we could plough grassland morning, noon and night whether it pissed with rain or whether it didn't.'

It was in 1942 that Jack got into blasting. 'We had to shift some bloody great stumps, six feet across. I had an HD 7 tractor, great big thing, and he couldn't push 'em out. Then someone said, "Look, Jack, there's an old boy down at Chichester, in Sussex — he'll blow 'em out for you."

'Next day, up come three of his chaps with a van, boxes of gelignite. I watched 'em. BOOM — up went the bloody lot. But he charged me ninety quid — and in those days that was a lot of money. I said, "Sod this for a box of tricks." Got onto ICI. They sent a man down, trained one of my chaps, and away we went, on stump-blowing and land clearance.'

Since then Hatts have progressed from blasting stumps to demolishing old chimneys and obsolete cooling towers. Jack confesses to a special weakness for felling chimneys. 'I love the nervous tension of it: you work through the five-minute hooter, the three-minute hooter, then one minute, ten seconds, and the final one, wondering all the time if your calculations are going to come right.'

Over the years, blasting techniques have been progressively refined. Jack's son Mark, now an acknowledged expert, does much work for film companies, and was once required to blow the wheels, engines and one wing off a Boeing 707 as it came down the runway — a feat which he managed without killing the two stunt pilots on board.

On the damming front, Hatts still blast out some duck ponds and lakes with explosive, but they excavate most with heavy machinery. At present the demand for new lakes it tremendous: everybody wants amenity water, for fishing, for boating or merely for contemplation.

'An inch of rain is 100 tons or 22,000 gallons to the acre,' Jack declares. 'Once you know that, you can work out anything you like.' Armed with this, and a thousand other essential facts about water, he travels the country advising landowners on matters hydraulic and piscatorial.

One memorable project was with the late Earl of Bradford, who had discovered what seemed to be an enormous lily pond at Shifnal, in Shropshire. Research in the Bodleian library and in Poland turned up the fact that the tank had been part of a carp farm.

A more recent visit was to Lord Salisbury, who is having problems with a lake at Hatfield. 'Charming old boy,' Jack found him. 'Great big feller, about 6' 5". Well over seventy. There he sits in his little old office at the back of his house. Trouble is, the lake won't hold water.'

Though still hard at work aged seventy-five, Jack finds time to shoot two days a week and fish the same. He keeps careful records of his sport: for every salmon or big sea-trout caught he has a wallpaper cut-out, traced round its shape and filled in at the time with its details. Thus he can tell you with confidence that his best-ever sea-trout was a 14¼ pounder. 'That was a lovely fish,' he says fondly. 'Caught about midnight — and didn't that bugger go! In the middle of the night. *Toof*!

But now he is off on how to make a rook pie (which he enjoys every year in May), about the delights of a harvest rabbit fried in breadcrumbs, about dew ponds ('There's no such thing'), about magpies, about the temperature underground, and the fact that he designed the water-jumps on every racecourse in England.

'Artful old sod,' he several times says of men with whom he has done business — and I do not feel he would be at all put out if I applied that phrase to him.

Cut-throat Elvering

In days of old, people in the villages along the Severn south of Gloucester would by now be beginning to enjoy their seasonal treat of a feed of elvers — for the baby eels are starting to swill up-river on the tide, having drifted by the million in the Gulf Stream from their distant spawning grounds in the Sargasso Sea.

When they enter the river, elvers are like translucent strips of pasta, and are known as 'glass eels' — about two inches long, 1,000 to a pound, with hearts, eyes and other organs visible in their gelatinous bodies. Senior citizens tell you how to cook them: fry them in home-cured bacon fat, add vinegar and pepper, break an egg into them and scramble it about — and there you are: a thoroughly satisfying dish with a slightly fishy taste all its own.

According to Les Coole, who farms at Frampton-on-Severn, elvers are also 'very potent'. A plump, stocky man now in his fifties, Les is something of an expert on the subject.

'The old tale was that women wouldn't cook 'em for their husbands,' he says, 'because there were more children got when the elvers were about than at any other time of year. But then birth control came in, and it went the other way round: the women used to go out looking for elvers for their husbands, to gee 'em up a bit!'

Half a century ago, before many people had cars and before anyone had a deep-freeze, elvering was a simple business. Local lads would go down to the river of an evening, take up a good position on the bank, and stand there holding a frame-net in the water. As the tide flooded in, the elvers would come with it, and sometimes, just at high water, the tiny eels would float to the sides of the river and mass together in the form of immense tubes or snakes, each several hundred yards long, and continue up-river in that packed formation just off the bank.

All an elverer had to do then was plunge his net through the middle of the shoal, and it would come up loaded every time. A catch of 200, 300 or even 400lb a night was by no means uncommon, and in the morning the fisherman would hawk it round his village by the bucketful, sometimes from an old cast-iron bath strapped on the back of a car, selling at maybe a shilling (5p) a pound, and feeding any left over to the chickens.

Elvers captured and kept alive produce what is known as 'vomp' — a frothy, protective slime, which tastes disgusting and takes a great deal of washing-off. When elvers were being caught for local consumption, the best way of preventing the formation of vomp was to put them into a pillow-case, inside a hessian sack, and screw the neck down tight, thus killing them quickly.

It was on the Green at Frampton, outside the Three Horseshoes, that the celebrated elver-eating contests began on Easter Monday more than twenty years ago. The first gastronomic competition — for the consumption of sausages — had started three years earlier, when the local coal merchant walked into Roger Broomhall the butcher, waving a newspaper cutting which related how a Cambridge student had eaten 2¾ lb of sausages in ten minutes and was claiming a world record.

'I could eat 'em faster than that,' said the coal merchant.

'Right', said Roger. 'Easter Monday on the Green, then. We'll have a contest.'

Eight entrants were supposed to turn out, but when one failed to show, Les Coole, who was helping cook the sausages, was persuaded to take his place — and promptly won. For the next four years he proved unbeatable, and reduced his time for eating 3 lb of sausages to eight minutes. As he says, he has always had a fair appetite, and took the precaution of downing a good fried breakfast before the contests, which began at 11 am.

During his reign he suggested that, because elvers were a local speciality, and in season at Easter, they should take the place of the sausages. So competitive elver-eating was born — and again Les won, earning a place in the *Guinness Book of Records* with his time of thirty-two seconds for a pound in 1972. Soon the event was attracting up to 2,000 spectators, and proceeds were used to give the old folk of the village a slap-up, sit-down meal.

But alas — the whole nature of elvering was being undermined by the appearance of wholesalers, or middlemen, who found that they could export the baby eels live for breeding or restocking to countries all over the world. From its original rustic level, the price climbed inexorably until it passed that of smoked salmon and almost rivalled that of caviar; and when, three years ago, it reached £20 a kilo, it knocked the elver-eating contest on the head.

By then, it is true, there had been a general reaction against exhibitions of gluttony, and eating records were expunged from the *Guinness Book of Records*. But Les Coole is adamant that it was the cost, rather than suggestions of bad taste, which finished the contests.

In the past few years, sky-high prices have drawn ever-increasing numbers of fishermen to the river bank. The National Rivers Authority now issues over 500 licences a year (at £20 apiece), and this season, for the first time, all licence-holders are required by law to have tags on their nets to confirm their identity. Also for the first time, fishermen are required to declare their catch to the NRA.

These innovations are part of the Authority's attempt to tighten its grip on eel stocks, for the paradox is that, while interest in elver-fishing has rocketed, catches have fallen disastrously over the past ten years. Amateurs blame overfishing, but experts such as Dr Alan Starkie of the NRA point out that a male eel takes seven years to reach maturity in the river, and a female fifteen, and that therefore even if high-pressure elver-fishing did set in about 1980, its effects could not become apparent until at least 1995.

Dr Starkie hopes that the decline may be no more than a natural, cyclical dip in population, which will right itself in due course. Meanwhile, the NRA is doing all it can to conserve stocks by buying elvers from Bristol Channel Fisheries, the largest of the commercial receiving stations, and releasing them up-river in areas which they would not otherwise reach.

Much about eels remains mysterious. Because elvers have only limited control over their movement in water — they can make themselves rise or fall by changing their buoyancy, but cannot steer — it seems impossible that they deliberately return, like salmon, to the river from which their parents came. It may thus be that the elvers now entering the Severn are not from Severn stock at all.

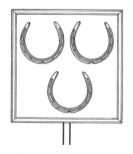

Meanwhile, elvering has degenerated from peaceful pastime to cut-throat competition. Instead of being spaced out, one every few hundred yards, fishermen stake their pitches on the bank hours before the tide comes in, and then stand shoulder to shoulder. Fights are commonplace.

On another front, Bristol Channel Fisheries are battling in court to protect people's age-old right to fish, which Gloucester County Council is trying to usurp. The Council has already suffered one defeat, when it claimed it actually owned the right, but now it is trying to block or ration access to the bank.

Worst of all for locals is the fact that almost the whole catch goes live for export, and people can no longer come by that potent feed which used to be such a cheerful harbinger of spring.

Lions in the Landscape

When the gates of Longleat safari park open for the summer next Saturday*, it will be exactly twenty-five years since the former trapeze artist, animal trainer and circus proprietor Jimmy Chipperfield realised his dearest ambition and let lions loose into the English landscape.

The notion of a zoo designed for cars is now so well established that its origins are easily forgotten; but the release of the big cats, and the opening of the park, were traumatic events, without precedent anywhere in the world. When Chipperfield first went to Longleat, to meet Lord Bath, his host kept him waiting for half an hour, and the circus man almost walked out — for he had a fetish about punctuality. Then, as he outlined his idea, Bath took some time to grasp it. 'Won't the cages have to be awfully big, if cars are to drive into them?' he asked — and his stocky little visitor said, 'No, no: it's the *people* who are going to be in the cages — their cars — and the lions are going to be free.'

Even Chipperfield, seasoned as he was, had no idea what would happen when the lions were first let out. In the event, the instant they touched down from their travelling wagons, they fought like fiends and bolted into the trees, lashing out at tussocks of grass with their paws. Chipperfield was immensely excited, and thought it the most marvellous sight he had ever seen — but he did not for the moment realise that the animals were terrified of the sky: having lived all their lives in cages, they were not used to the huge, high canopy above them, and they sought reassurance by going to the nearest stretch of fence — something with which they were familiar — and pacing up and down it.

Luckily for the organisers, while the venture was being planned, *The Times* had lost its head and run an editorial denouncing the scheme as a 'dangerous

* 15 March 1991

folly'. Calling it a 'quite gratuitous and unnecessary risk to life', the paper had called for its suppression. This tirade stimulated interest splendidly, and when the park opened, at Easter 1966, public curiosity was overwhelming.

The home team — principally Jimmy Chipperfield, his son Richard, his daughter Mary and her husband Roger Cawley — hardly knew what had hit them. For the whole of Good Friday, every road approaching the entrance was jammed solid with cars, and it was the same on Easter Monday. Lord Bath himself came out on to the gates with a satchel, collecting money with enthusiasm.

Inside the park, chaos threatened, for there too the lines of crawling vehicles seized up. The two-way radios ordered for the wardens had failed to arrive, so that it was almost impossible for the staff to find out what was happening in different parts of the reserve. In that one weekend, 3,000 cars went through, and, even at a charge of only £1 per car, the takings were such that the Chipperfields saw they had struck gold. Business was so good, in fact, that by September they had paid off the entire capital cost of the enterprise.

Twenty-five years on, the lions of Longleat are still flourishing. Jimmy Chipperfield died last year, but the enterprise is still owned fifty/fifty by his family and Lord Bath, and still run by his son-in-law, Roger Cawley. The gloomy predictions of *The Times* were confounded; in quarter of a century millions of people have driven through the lion reserve, and not one has been bitten, let alone killed. No lions have escaped and established themselves ineradicably in the fastnesses of the Welsh mountains (as another prophet of doom feared they would).

The only serious accident occurred in the 1970s, when a chimpanzee called Fred somehow got ashore from his island in the lake and attacked the keeper who tried to recapture him. The man was so badly bitten that both his hands had to be amputated.

Otherwise, things have gone well, and Chipperfield's idea has proved exceedingly durable. The original twelve-foot wire-mesh fences still encircle the 100-acre lion reserve; the original wooden posts are still in position. No lions survive from the earliest days — for, living in groups, as they do here, they have a life-span of only about ten years; but the latter-day denizens behave in exactly the same way as the pioneers.

By no means tame, they have clearly defined rules of conduct. They regard the roads as alien ground, and so long as cars remain on the tarmac, take no interest in them. But everything off the road is lion territory, and if any car intrudes on that, they surround it immediately. Should a human get out of his vehicle, he would be attacked at once.

The lions have long since been reinforced by other species. Baboons did so much damage to cars that they were replaced by rhesus monkeys. Giraffes, zebras, elephants, rhinos and Ankole cattle all joined early; later came tigers, camels and wolves. The lake, with its sealions and hippos, and gorillas on an island, became an attraction on its own (the gorillas have a centrally-heated house, with television permanently switched on).

Over the years the staff have witnessed some amazing incidents — not least one in which a tiger leapt at a kestrel which had tried to pinch a bit of its meat, and knocked the bird down, ripping out its tail. A keeper reached the hawk quickly enough to save it, and over the next few weeks nursed it back to health.

During the lifetime of the park, animal values have changed enormously. In 1966, Jimmy Chipperfield had to scour the world to find fifty lions. Today — largely as the result of his own invention — they are two-a-penny, and many of the Longleat lionesses are given hormone implants to prevent them breeding.

Gorillas, in contrast, are priceless and impossible to buy above board. Even an animal of dubious origins would cost £100,000. Elephants, both African and Asian, are almost as difficult to find: hence the fervent hopes that the Longleat group will start breeding soon.

Another marked change is in the attitude of traditional zoos. When Chipperfield launched his concept, the establishment turned its back on him, and of all the zoo-directors whom he invited to his official opening, only one deigned to accept. Today, there is widespread recognition that safari parks can play a useful role as reservoirs of endangered species, and when British zoos recently exported a herd of Pere David deer, to re-start the species in China, Longleat contributed six of the animals. Besides, the Chipperfields are recognised as expert transporters of animals, and if someone wants to shift an elephant or a rhino across the country, it is very often to them that he comes.

Inevitably, the animals at Longleat are now backed up by the kind of entertainments considered essential for such a resort — miniature railway, adventure playground in the shape of an immense castle, *Dr Who* exhibition, restaurant, and the biggest maze in the world. Yet it is still the lions which exert the strongest attraction and pull in 500,000 visitors a year.

Like his late father-in-law, Roger Cawley is a showman to his boots, and must always have a new attraction. This year's is Carla, a white lioness from South Africa. An independent observer feels bound to report that her colour is a rather *creamy* shade of white; but for all that, she is a spectacular animal, and a fitting emblem of this summer's silver jubilee.

Sir Vauncey's Passion

The moment you enter the hall, you know you have come to an enclave of eccentricity, for you are instantly eye-ball-to-eye-ball with an array of huge stuffed heads. Are they buffalo or oxen or some rare breed of cattle? It is hard to say: huge horns curve down so that they almost meet beneath the throat, black eyes glare.

And what is this? An ornate stove, standing out away from the wall, full of logs blazing merrily, *but without a chimney*? Ah yes, somebody explains: the flue goes down the back, under the floor, and up outside.

But wait: the hall is only a small room. It is the magnificent saloon, two storeys high, that packs the knock-out punch. Never mind the pictures, or the splendid proportions of the room, which dwarf a grand piano. Look at the birds: case after case full of stuffed pheasants, owls, hawks, sea-birds . . . and, among a thousand other natural curiosities, the skull of a crocodile.

This is Calke Abbey, near Derby, which the National Trust will open to the public for the first time at Easter: an astonishing treasure-house hidden away in the folds of a lovely park near Derby. Since 1622 it has belonged to the Harpur family, and partly by luck, partly thanks to an immensely skilled rescue operation, its interior and contents have scarcely changed in the past 100 years.

An agreeable strain of eccentricity has run deep in the family for generations. Sir Henry Harpur (who inherited in 1789, and added the Crewe to his name) was so reclusive that he became known as the Isolated Baronet. Acute shyness led him to communicate with his servants and children in writing. In the evenings, though his table was set with several places, he would dine alone, allowing no servant to appear in the room.

Indeed, the house and its environs were laid out so that the servants might be seen as little as possible. Tunnels connect the old kitchen with the brewhouse and the stables, and indoors the passages are arranged so that the staff could go about their work without entering the main rooms.

Sir Henry did overcome his inhibitions enough to scandalise neighbours by marrying his mistress, Annette Hawkins, a lady's maid; and perhaps his union with an outsider drove the bashful genes underground for a couple of generations; but they surfaced again strongly in the person of his great-grandson Sir Vauncey Harpur Crewe (1846–1924), whose obsession with natural history led him to close his 1,000-acre park to outsiders, to let the whole area run riot, and to shoot and stuff every creature which came within range.

Aided and abetted by his head-keeper Agathos Pegg, he prowled his purlieus constantly, armed with a gun, which he put down only when he went to church on Sundays and stood the weapon in the porch. Since he did not like motor cars, he forbade any to enter the park. Guests came and went in horse-drawn carriages, which met them at the lodge; and the post travelled in the same fashion, outgoing letters being placed in a bag on the billiard-table, whence the butler would collect them and start them on their journey to the outside world.

It was Sir Vauncey's ungovernable passion for collecting that filled the house not merely with birds by the hundred, but with thousands of other natural objects — minerals, shells, bones, eggs, flowers, grasses. Even now the lobby to what was his office is boiling with foxes and otters, one of them holding a twenty-pound pike. Yet it was also his dislike of change which so miraculously froze the interior in its late-Victorian state.

When Sir Vauncey's grandson Charles died intestate in 1981, he left his younger brother Henry a bill for death-duties of £8 million. With no mean courage, Henry took the decision to transfer the house and 1,000 acres of land to the National Trust. Now, after four years of repairs, and the expenditure of £3,500,000, the future of Calke is secure — and the Trust, it seems to me, has pulled off a brilliant feat, in that, although it had to carry out extensive renovations (including the replacement of the entire roof), it has managed to leave the house looking almost exactly as it was, outside and in, not even redecorating most of the rooms. To walk into the library, the drawing room or the saloon is like being whisked back a century into another world.

Henry Harpur Crewe — a small, friendly man, of wayward charm, now sixty-eight and at only a slight angle to the universe — has moved into a flat on the ground floor. He is naturally a little nervous about the impending invasion by the masses, and cannot help thinking of the past.

'Funny, this old barn,' he said, as we had lunch in the spacious new restaurant. 'We used to have hay in here, and in there —' he pointed through some arches into an elegant alcove — 'we kept the chickens.' Then, as he saw me gathering up some plates, with scraps of lettuce and potato skins on them, he said, 'What a waste!'

Today, the herd of red and fallow deer are confined to one area of the park. Once, they used to roam all round the house. 'That was much nicer,' said the last of the Harpur Crewes. 'In the old days, I'd have just thrown that stuff out of the window, and the deer would have gobbled it up in no time.'

Valley Where Time Stood Still

Several times in past years, as March has drawn to its close, I have toyed with the idea of writing an April fool fantasy about a country house, long lost to the world, which has suddenly come back from the dead.

I thought about the place so often that I could see it plainly: a stately pile, Georgian or Regency, crumbling away at the head of its park, half-hidden by ancient yews and cedars. By some mysterious alchemy — the lie of its encircling hills, the lack of roads, the deep woods, the direction of prevailing wind and light — it had hardly ever been seen by strangers, and had remained cut off from the outside world.

Perhaps there was an even more curious reason for the fact that people had forgotten it. Perhaps, in the 1920s, the owner had wielded sufficient influence with the cartographers of the Ordnance Survey to have all trace of it erased from their charts, so that modern maps showed the patch of country round it as a blank.

For the past fifty years, in any case, the estate had been owned by a spinster, who had gradually given up farming and forestry. Now at last she had died, in her nineties, leaving the place in the hands of executors, who wished to sell it privately, without demeaning themselves by having a brochure printed . . .

Each year my fantasy acquired a few more trappings — but then suddenly, just as 1 April was coming round again, in the most extraordinary way life imitated art. Not only did I find that my dream estate existed: I went by invitation of the new owner to walk round it, and found it every bit as derelict and fantastical as my imagination had suggested.

To preserve some element of mystery, let us call the estate simply X. It straddles the borders of Wiltshire and Hampshire. Of its 2,000 acres, some 450 are farmed, but the rest have simply run wild.

It is true that the house — a handsome Regency building, dating from 1810 — is less remote and in better condition than I imagined, but it does stand at the head of a derelict park; it is half-hidden by yews and cedars, and for more than forty years it was inhabited by a spinster, who died last year at the age of ninety-two. Still stranger, it was never formally put on the market, but sold privately by the old lady's executors.

Today the big, airy rooms are empty, but the tall windows command phenomenal views to the south — it is said that one can see the ships in Southampton Water, thirty miles away. The house's proportions are those of a more leisured age, and printed notices still proclaim that, in the event of fire, it is the duty of 'the indoor servants' to initiate evacuation procedures.

But the great glory of X is its astonishing hidden valley. Walk down the park, past shattered oaks, limes and the odd, rather stunted monkey-puzzle tree, turn left at the bottom, and you enter a world in which time seems to have been arrested generations ago.

Together with the new owner and other friends, I walked there on a day of wild west wind. Hail showers swept over us from time to time, but gleams of sun came flying in behind them, to light up a scene of quite magical dereliction.

Down the middle of the valley lay a wide stretch of uncultivated grass, dun-coloured, with no new growth yet showing through; and above the grass, on either side, ran woods of a wildness not easily described. Hazel, once coppiced but untouched for years, sprouted in dense profusion. Thorn bushes had established impenetrable thickets, some of them acres in extent.

The most amazing natural phenomena were the yew trees which grew high on the stony banks. Without cutting one down, we could not determine their age, but they must have been several hundred years old, with trunks three or four feet in diameter, and their canopies extending all round to form perfect circles thirty or more yards across. From a distance, each tree looked like a whole clump, such were its dimensions.

Already primroses were shining in the grass, and later, no doubt, there will be cowslips and orchids. In summer, I am sure that the grass will be alive with butterflies, which flourish on ground never sprayed with chemicals.

From out of the primeval cover on our left three roebucks came bounding, down one side of the valley and up the other in line-ahead formation. Overhead, two buzzards circled, loosing off high whistles. I was not surprised to learn that what had clinched matters for my friend, and made him decide to buy the place, was the fact that when during his first visit he stopped for a moment to answer a call of nature, four woodcock took off almost from under his feet.

If I had not seen it, I would never have believed that such an estate could still exist in the south of England. It reminded me of the Tyneham valley at Lulworth, in Dorset, which has been abandoned uncultivated since the army took it over as a gunnery range during the second world war.

Tyneham has the same shaggy, unkempt look, the same tussocky grass and rioting blackthorn. But whereas that landscape has been frozen by the presence of the military, the valley at X has stayed the way it is through benign negligence, or even through a positive desire to keep things as they are. (I am not sure what the old lady's motives were, but I suspect that she simply did not notice how her estate had got away from her.)

Yet the dereliction must be far older than her tenure of the land: those yews, for instance, have not been touched for centuries. What I found most fascinating was the absence of any sign that man had ever inhabited the valley. Not only were there no roads or fences or walls between fields: there were no cottages, no barns, not even any ruins to show where buildings had once stood. The reason may have been the lack of water on that high downland — but whatever the cause, the result was wonderful.

Perhaps it was because we were not far from the great prehistoric shrines of Stonehenge and Avebury that fantasies began to build in my mind. Such was the feeling of timelessness that I half expected a wolf to appear out of the thicket in pursuit of the roe; and if, in a clearing, we had come on small, hirsute humans, clad in skins and chipping away at flints, it would hardly have been a surprise.

As we walked, I could not but wonder what I would do with the estate if it were mine. I am by nature an improver: if I see run-down land or buildings, I immediately start thinking what satisfaction could be got from putting them to rights.

Yet in that lost valley my reforming zeal very soon evaporated. A fanatical improver could easily spend millions there: he could rip out the thorn with bulldozers, clear up, burn, plant proper trees, restore some land to agriculture, fence the fields . . . and yet what would all that gain? Farm crops would not produce worthwhile yields on such stony soil; deer, rabbits, hares and squirrels would eat the young trees. Nothing would be achieved except the destruction of a unique environment.

I am glad to report that the new owner of X feels the same as I do. As it happens, he could well afford to carry out the most brutal reformation of the landscape. But, as it also happens, he is by some miracle a man who hankers after wildness, and he intends to leave things very much as they are.

Monarch of the Sky

Going out into the garden after lunch, I heard a piercing clamour of seagulls, coming from far away. At once I sensed that the noise was different from the normal squabbling conversation which rises from a flock following the plough: these cries were wild and desperate, prophesying doom.

At first I thought that the birds must be mobbing a fox, which maybe had caught one of them out on a field to the west. But, as I looked down the valley, I could see nothing: then I realised that the cacophony was high in the sky, and coming my way.

Gazing up, I spotted the gulls, at a tremendous height: to the naked eye they were no more than wisps and gleams of white, flashing and disappearing against the deep blue sky. Half a minute later I had them in a pair of 10 x 50 binoculars: hundreds of them, wheeling frenziedly in bright sunshine, at least 1,500 feet up, all screaming.

What was it that had put them in such fear and sent them to such an altitude? A moment later I had the answer. Into the ring of my glasses sailed the majestic form of a peregrine, gliding in huge, easy circles halfway between me and the gulls.

The hair on my neck rose at the sight of it. Normally the finest hawk we can muster is a buzzard; but a buzzard, with its blunt-ended wings and laboured flight, is a heavyweight plodder, and not in the same league as this princely intruder. With its wings curved back in the shape of a scimitar, and a bar of dark brown showing across the feathers of its fanned-out tail, it swung through the sky with awe-inspiring ease and certainty.

Clearly it was travelling, rather than hunting. It could, had it so wished, have climbed among the seagulls and knocked down any one of them in a puff of feathers; but it was merely circling on set wings in enormous, effortless sweeps, and at the same time letting the wind carry it towards the east.

There was something magnificent about the scale of its progress. By its mere passage, without lifting a feather, it had terrified every seagull in the county. From its altitude, our valley must have looked no more than a furrow in the ground, the escarpment a mere wrinkle on the face of the earth.

As I watched, I had time to wonder where it had come from. I think it was a young bird, perhaps hatched last year at Symonds Yat, in the Forest of Dean, to the south-west of us. Maybe it was wandering in search of a mate. Clearly it had just crossed the Severn estuary, for that must have been where it picked up its screeching escort. As for its destination — who could say? The soft lowlands of central southern England, for which it was heading, are not peregrine territory.

No matter. To have seen it was enough. In two or three minutes it had vanished over the hill, but it left my head ringing with biblical phrases. Certainly that great bird was making the clouds its chariot, and walking upon the wings of the wind: to me it was the spirit of the sky — and to the gulls it was the very instrument, if not the angel, of death.

★   ★   ★

No wonder the *Mary Rose* sank like a stone when she turned turtle off Portsmouth on 19 July 1545. She was, it is true, carrying a great weight of guns, equipment and men, but I now feel sure that, even without her extra burdens, the sheer mass of the oak from which she was built would have taken her to the bottom.

I say 'now', because for the past couple of months I have been battling with the trunk of an immense oak, and feel I have gained special insights into the nature of the wood. This tree is reckoned to have been at least 500 years old, and so, if the estimate is correct, must have been growing in my neighbour's field when Henry VIII's flagship capsized.

No one seems sure how many years have passed since the oak fell down: ten, at least, and somebody long ago set fire to the roots and cut off all the branches, so that the hulk is dead as dead can be. By now most other kinds of timber would have rotted away to pulp or powder: not this.

The strength and resilience of the wood are astonishing: the grain, veering all ways where branches once sprouted from the trunk, makes it a brute to split, and chunks fly the length of a cricket pitch as they part company from the main body, such is the violence needed to dislodge them.

Yet still more extraordinary are the weight of the wood and the amount of water it contains. Moisture spurts out at the impact of the axe, and even lumps of moderate size easily break the hundredweight barrier. One day, as I was unloading a trailer-full of hard-won pieces, one fell into a water-tank and, far from floating, plummeted into the depths.

As so many seasons have passed since my tree was alive, the moisture in its trunk can only be rain; and, in an attempt to gauge the wood's powers of absorption, I have started a modest experiment. I have weighed one twenty-pound lump now, and will weigh it again in a year's time, to see how much of its mass has evaporated.

In my woodshed about five tons of oak are gently giving back their moisture to the air. But whenever I go in there and smell the wood's sweet, nutty scent, I think of the poor *Mary Rose,* and her sodden timbers, and the 700 men who went with her to the bottom of the sea.

April

Argonauts at Large

The 1990 Macallan Argo Grand Prix, which starts from the West Highland port of Mallaig at nine o'clock tomorrow morning, 1 April, promises to be the most spectacular race of its kind so far. It is fitting that on this, its tenth anniversary, the event should have attracted the highest entry to date: thirty-one two-man teams, all of them lured by the record prize money: £10,000 for the winners, £5,000 for second and £2,500 for third.

For the benefit of anyone not familiar with the Argo, I should explain that it is a splendid little all-terrain vehicle, whose low-pressure tyres (six or eight, according to the model, and all driven) enable it to tackle any kind of ground. On the flat its top speed is only 18mph, but on steep slopes, heather, mud, sand, peat-bogs and snow it is in a class of its own. It is also fully amphibious, although when afloat it is propelled only by the treads of its Runamuk tyres, turning like paddles, and so makes somewhat painfully slow headway.

Built in Canada and imported into Britain in kit form, the vehicle is assembled here. Comfort is *not* its strong suit, since the body consists of a hard polyethylene tub, and accommodation is basic. So are the controls: the driver has no steering wheel or clutch, but manages his roaring steed with a hand-grip throttle and two brake levers, left and right, which, if yanked with sufficient violence, can turn the vehicle through ninety or even 180 degrees in its own length. Skid-steering, they call it.

Primitive as they may sound, today's Argos are a good deal more polished than their predecessors. They have bigger engines (four-stroke instead of two), and better transmission. I have vivid memories of riding in the back of an early model when suddenly the sheep-dog that I was cradling in my arms leapt clean overboard with a penetrating yelp, having had the last two inches of its tail severed by one of the drive-chains. Such accidents, I am glad to say, are no longer possible; and the wretched shear-pins, which used constantly to live up to their name by breaking, are also a thing of the past.

The point about Argos in Scotland is that they have become firm favourites with everyone who works in the hills. Foresters use them for transporting seedlings, wire and fence-posts to distant plantations, farmers cart hay and sheep-nuts in them and deer-stalkers rely heavily on them for bringing down the carcases of animals culled high in the mountains.

It was this last fact that put the idea of the Argo Grand Prix, coast to coast, into the mind of the whisky magnate Sir Moray Macallan. He instituted the event in 1981 and his theory that deer-stalkers would prove the canniest and most tenacious drivers has been proved right time and again: of the nine races held so far, stalkers have won no fewer than seven.

Yet there was another element behind Sir Moray's patronage: his enthusiasm for what the Victorians called 'pedestrianism'. Himself no mean walker — he once ascended sixteen Munros, or 3,000-foot summits, in twenty-four hours — he resembles that great eccentric Sir John Astley in his predilection for inciting others to cover great distances on foot.

So it was that, for the first Argo races, he specified the Highland equivalent of a Le Mans start: when the gun went, competitors had to cover five miles of gruelling terrain on foot before beginning to drive. This, as he hoped, sorted out the townies and gave the true hill-men a flying send-off.

For tomorrow, however, there is an important innovation. To improve the spectacle for television, competing vehicles will line up on the football field at Mallaig and drive from there in a mass take-off. The sight will be a stirring one, for it has become standard practice to decorate the stumpy little Argos — normally red or green — with painted eyes, teeth, feathers and so on, and competition to reach open ground first will mean rough tactics.

One unique feature of the race is that there is no set route. Entrants have to collect tokens from a series of check-points, but between these isolated spots they choose their own way, even crossing lochs if they think it feasible. The only major prohibition is that although they may *cross* tarmac roads, they may not drive along them.

From Mallaig, the line of advance lies due east along the rocky spine of North Morar — itself no mean obstacle. The pedestrian stage comes on the mountain known as Sgurr-na-Ciche, whose conical peak towers 3,400 feet above the eastern end of Loch Nevis: even an Argo cannot negotiate slopes as steep as those of the last 1,000 feet, and competitors will have to leg the final precipitous stretch to the check-point on the summit.

Thereafter the Argos will grind on through the wilds of Lochaber, cross the Great Glen at Laggan and swing north-eastwards through the Monadhliath mountains until they come to the head-waters of the River Findhorn, and so make their way down to the finish at Findhorn Bay on the Moray Firth.

The race is first and foremost a test of physical endurance, for on rough terrain the Argo fairly flings its occupants around; but it is also a supreme test of map-reading and of a man's eye for ground. The drivers can never relax, for they have to steer every inch of the way. Fuel is obtainable at dumps airlifted to the check-points, but competitors have to carry their own food, drink and spares.

The hardiest — among them last year's winners, the brothers Hector and Biffo Kennedy from Drumnadrochit — drive right through the night and hope to complete the course in under forty hours. But if the mist comes down — as it has twice in the past — everyone is brought to a standstill.

The risks, of course, are considerable: four or five Argos are written off every year, usually in ravines or steep-sided burns, and one or two generally sink. But full insurance is now compulsory and medical facilities have been much improved. Not only must all vehicles carry radios and Sarbe (search-and-rescue beacons), but there are helicopters on standby to lift out casualties.

With a fresh fall of snow on the high ground, and the burns in spate, the Kennedy brothers are odds-on favourites to win again; but even if they do, the rest will not be too discouraged, for besides the three main prizes, there are generous consolation awards: every crew to finish receives a case of the sponsors' matchless and rarely seen twenty-five-year-old malt whisky.

Speaking of notable spring occasions, tomorrow also brings that other highlight, the annual rat-shoot in the cellars of Harrods, in which the vermin are driven, block by block, to a team of seven crack guns wielding double-barrelled .410s.

I am delighted to report that, after my earlier description of the event in this column, interest was so strong that pellet-proof Perspex screens have been erected to form viewing galleries and that this year the public will be admitted for the first time.

I should, however, warn any prospective spectators that visibility may not be that good, as the automatic fire-systems have to be switched off for the duration of the shoot and cordite smoke is liable to hang in the air. But anyone keen should be outside the Hans Crescent entrance by 6.30am.

At £50 each, tickets are not cheap, but you do get fresh orange juice thrown in — and anyway, has not Harrods' motto always been 'Never knowingly oversold'?

High Jinks in Hungerford

'BITE HIM IN THE LEG!' roared the Vicar. 'Get him with your teeth — now!'

The advice was sound enough, for his wife's jaws were within reach of one of her attackers' calves; but the odds against her were too heavy, and anyway she had other preoccupations — such as vainly trying to keep her skirt down (or, when she was inverted, up) at a decent level, and she had no chance of escape until the blacksmith had driven a nail home into the heel of her shoe.

Elsewhere on the floor of the Corn Exchange other victims were bellowing like bulls as assailants pitched into them, and shrieks of laughter were punctuated by the merry crash of tables being overthrown. In other words, the annual Hocktide festivities in the Berkshire country town of Hungerford were reaching their traditional climax.

An extraordinary pagan survival, Hocktide has been observed in Hungerford for at least 500 years, and probably much longer. Local historians claim that it began in celebration of Ethelred's victory over the Danes in 1002 AD, or even in Roman times.

Whatever its origin, it is closely bound up with the town's unique form of local government, which derives directly from a long association with John o' Gaunt, Duke of Lancaster, in the fourteenth century. A friend and frequent guest of Sir Thomas Hungerford (first Speaker in Parliament), the Duke is thought to have stayed in the area on and off for twenty years, and, in return for local support, granted the commoners fishing rights in the rivers Kennet and Dun. To these, later, were added rights of grazing cattle and picking watercress on the common, and still, to this day, jealously-guarded rights are attached to ninety-nine properties in the town.

Hocktide — the Monday and Tuesday of the second week after Easter — is the season at which the officers of the Town and Manor review the past year and set in hand arrangements for the months ahead. This year, as ever, the mixture of ritual and carousing began with the Macaroni Supper, held on the Friday after Easter at the John O'Gaunt Inn by the Constable and his officers of the Hocktide Court. As always, the macaroni was accompanied by watercress and jugs of ale.

Yet the big day was Tuesday — Tuttiday, so called (people think) after a West Country word meaning a bunch of flowers. Certainly flowers were much in evidence when your correspondent — kindly invited as the Guest of Honour — arrived in the High Street at mid-morning: many of the elegant, red-brick houses sported floral decorations, and others were hung with blue and yellow ribbons.

It soon became evident that the main problem would be to remain sober enough to make a speech after lunch, for in almost every building a party was going on, and every time I moved or opened my mouth I was offered another drink by some perfect stranger.

Meanwhile, down the west side of the High Street, a posse of roisterers was making erratic progress. The two Tuttimen, in morning dress, with red roses of Lancaster in their buttonholes, were exacting kisses and money from the ladies in every common house, ascending ladders if necessary to collar their prey, and being refreshed with drinks at every stop.

Each of them carried a tutti pole or stave, swathed in blue ribbons, thickly encrusted with yellow flowers, and topped by an orange — a reference to the occasion when Prince William of Orange passed through the town. With them came the Orangeman, a stout and commanding figure also in morning dress, but with pheasants' tail-feathers sprouting vertically from his top hat and a sack of spare fruit over his shoulder. He too kissed every female in sight. Round him milled a scrum of children who scuffled and fought after any small change that fell loose.

Jolly as it was, the scene evoked far-flung echoes — of 'The Golden Bough', of the Pied Piper, and not least of Lewis Carroll. I had just thought, 'This looks like a party of snark-hunters,' when up hove none other than the Bellman — a splendid figure in black frock coat with scarlet cuffs and piping and a black topper braided with gold.

The sun came out. Alcohol levels rose steadily. One of the Tuttimen, it was reliably reported, had already downed twenty-seven whiskies. Someone told me that the Orangeman was a retired coalman. A troop of Morris dancers came clumping up the street and cavorted outside the Town Hall to the strains of 'The British Grenadiers'.

Inside, at a reception given by my host the Constable, Dennis Cryer, a genial accountant who turns the scales at nineteen stone, I fell into conversation with the Bellman, Robin Tubb. His family have held the office for more than 100 years, and he himself is in his thirty-fourth season. The horn with which he roused the burghers at 8 am that morning dates (he told me) from 1634, but this is only the *new* horn, and the old one, given by John o'Gaunt himself, is kept in safe custody.

By 1 pm more than 150 flushed commoners and their guests had taken their places in the high and handsome Corn Exchange, and we of the top table processed in to a massed, rhythmic handclap. Before anything could be drunk, the Constable invited his two official Ale Tasters to pronounce on the quality of the beer set before us. Rising to their feet with huge pewter tankards, they solemnly declared the ale to be of excellent quality.

So it was. So was the lunch. Roars of applause greeted the Constable when he announced that, by some oversight, the printers had given us last year's menu instead of this. No matter. Time passed at amazing speed. Before me, at one stage, stood glasses of ale, red and white wine and port. Then, as if these needed reinforcement, along came steaming silver bowls of Plantagenate Punch, brewed to a secret recipe, in which we drank toasts to 'the Queen, Duke of Lancaster' and sundry others.

Next came the speeches. Somehow I staggered through mine. But the climax came when, during the fourth and last oration, there was a sudden, earth-shaking crash from one end of the hall and the Bellman toppled sideways to the floor. The accident was in no way his fault — his chair-leg had caught in a heating duct — but it brought the house down.

I had been warned what would happen next, but somehow was not ready for it. I was chatting agreeably to the Vicar when suddenly powerful young men appeared on either hand and seized me by the arms. Instinctively I tried to fight them off. I made some progress. We crashed headlong over the table. But then two more got me by the legs, and I was borne to the floor and pinned there while the blacksmith hammered a silvery horseshoe into the heel of one shoe. Only when I yelled 'Punch!', signifying that I was willing to pay for my share of the Plantagenate brew, was I allowed back on my feet.

A general riot, good natured but violent, broke out as one by one the other colts, or newcomers, were seized and shod: girls, ladies, grandfathers — nobody was allowed to escape. When things quietened down, about six o'clock, it was time to roll out to the John o'Gaunt for anchovies on toast — and of course, more ale to wash them down.

That was enough for me. But the Tuttimen were still on their rounds, which did not end before they lurched back to their start-point, the Three Swans, at 9 pm; and as to whether they had to go home in their traditional conveyances — wheelbarrows — I felt it would be indelicate to inquire.

Bubbling Blackcock

It came at 5.25 am with the first glimmer of dawn: a long, bubbling call which carried clearly over the dark moor. 'He's there!' whispered my companion. 'Right on schedule.'

All round us, well back on the horizon, the mountains of North Wales rose black against the sky. Frost crunched in the grass underfoot, and a keen north-easterly breeze knifed into the backs of our necks as we huddled on a plank-bench in a skimpy hide; but minor discomforts were of no consequence, for out there in front of us a blackcock had come to his lek, or mating ground, and was starting his age-old ritual.

Blackgame are nearly double the size of red grouse, and the female, or greyhen, strongly resembles her smaller cousins, being barred and freckled in much the same combination of brown, buff and grey. The cock, however, is a more splendid creature altogether: glossy blue-black, with lyre-shaped tail-feathers turning outwards, white under-tail coverts, white flashes on his wings, and red wattles above his eyes.

Black grouse were once common in many English counties, but now they survive only in the north, in Scotland and a few parts of North Wales. Essentially birds of the upland forest edge, they need heather moors flanked by extensive woodland which contains plenty of openings and boggy patches — a combination increasingly rare.

In North Wales, their numbers are thought to have fallen to a total of only about 400, and determined efforts are now being made by the Forestry Commission, with help from the Royal Society for the Protection of Birds, to arrest their decline. Hence my dawn vigil this week, in the company of Mike Conway, the Commission's conservation ranger for Dolgellau forest district, who is making a survey of the birds in his area.

As he remarked, not many people would willingly get up before dawn to sit still for a couple of hours in the hope that a few birds would come and perform in front of them. But for him, and for me, it was magical to watch daybreak steal over the mountains.

Gradually the eastern sky paled until the stars went out; but for a while the land remained dark, and although we could hear the blackcock bubbling, we could not see him. Then at last light seemed to filter down to ground level, and details of the landscape stood revealed.

We were in a wide bowl, with ridges forming an irregular rim round the skyline. Up there, 1,250 feet above sea level, the plantation of sitka spruce was uneven: many of the young trees had died and disappeared, leaving open patches of grass and heather.

It was on one of these that the blackcock had alighted: a mound carpeted with tussocky grass 100 yards in front of us. At the height of last year's lek, in May (Mike told me), eight cock birds occupied this territory all at once; this year, so far, only two had shown up.

In the older trees behind us, songbirds struck up their dawn chorus. The light strengthened. Now, through binoculars, I could see the solid black shape of our first customer on the mound, moving erratically as he went into his song-and-dance routine.

For much of the time he prowled about in a crouching posture, with wings half extended, head held low and forward — and it was in this mode that he uttered his bubbling song. Then, every few minutes, with an abrupt screech or squawk, he would suddenly leap into the air, fly up to a height of three or four feet, and tumble down again.

No two of these explosive take-offs were quite the same. Some carried him a few yards across country; others landed him back where he had started. As Mike graphically put it, 'Sometimes he seems to fly up tidy, but sometimes he goes up all shapes.' Clearly he thought himself a hell of a fellow — and so he was; but what was the aim of his extraordinary dance?

To attract females, was the obvious answer. Yet there seemed to be no greyhen within miles. Mike whispered that females did not normally come to the lek so early in the season, but that if another male arrived, the two would instantly fight.

The sun crawled over the horizon behind us and cast a faint but welcome glow on our backs. In its pink radiance our solitary performer looked even more splendid, wattles blazing scarlet, plumage gleaming blue-black. Then I saw the point of his crouching stance. Every time he turned away from us, with his main tail curled over his back, his white under-tail flashed like a snowy beacon. I thought of great bustards, which, to attract females, inflate their white gular sacks so that they show up like giant puffballs. Our fellow was using slightly different means to achieve a similar end.

Yet why, in that case, had he not chosen a more rewarding site? His mound did not command particularly wide views, and there were many more prominent hillocks from which he could have flaunted his charms.

In low voices we discussed whether the birds are drawn to the same leks year after year by primeval instincts, as deer are drawn to rutting stands, or whether they choose any open space that takes their fancy. Mike was inclined to the second view, for he had noticed that blackcock sometimes lek on forestry rides or other man-made openings which have not been available to them before.

In fact, he reckoned, they move around as changes in the pattern of the forest dictate — and indeed the Commission's present programme of habitat-improvement consists mainly of maintaining or increasing the number of desirable open spaces, by removing trees and cutting grass and heather.

After a slow start, action broke out all around us. A movement on the skyline caught our eyes. Some 400 yards off, a second blackcock landed on a hillock and began to perform silhouetted on the horizon. From somewhere out of sight to our right came the bubbling of a third male. Then from our left floated the call of the year's first cuckoo, hot from Africa, and almost at the same moment a barn owl came faltering and feinting across our front only a few feet off the ground.

A fourth blackcock sped in, straight as a black arrow, and landed on the main lek. At once — as Mike had predicted — he and the original incumbent began to spar, circling warily in their ritual crouch, head to head, and flying up to strike at each other like farmyard cockerels. But the contest was more of a formality than a threat to either combatant, and the main effect of it was to advertise their presence still more boldly, for their upturned backsides flashed white signals which must have been visible half a mile away.

Soon they produced results. In swept a solitary greyhen, which plummeted into the heather a few yards from the brawlers. One of them immediately began posturing in her direction, but he seemed to have no serious intention of mating with her, and soon returned to his boxing.

Then, at about 7.15 — again exactly as Mike had forecast — both males decided they had had enough for the morning, and flew off to a breakfast of fresh heather-shoots. Stiff and half-frozen, we slipped away along a little stream, back to the road and home.

Never did bacon and eggs taste better; but as I ate them, my mind was till on those lovely birds and their mysterious rituals. That courtly dance is thousands of years old; and the question now is whether we can manage the upland environment with sufficient skill for it to survive through centuries to come.

Jarkemen and Patricoes

As Armada fever builds up with the approach of the four hundredth anniversary (in the summer of 1988) my mind dwells more and more on the question of what the English countryside was like in 1588. Far wilder than now, is the short answer: the population of England, Wales and Scotland was less than five million, the towns were infinitely smaller, and villages were cut off from each other by tracts of natural forest.

Communications scarcely existed. There were no newspapers as we now know them, and no post except the royal mail, which carried only Government correspondence. Roads were so bad, especially in winter, that travellers often forsook them and rode their horses by whatever route they could find across the fields. The result was that news travelled slowly, if at all, and although the system of warning beacons sent word of the Armada's arrival flashing through the kingdom during the last days of July, it must have taken weeks for people living far inland to find out what had happened in the battle.

Yet if much was different, some things were curiously the same. The weather was exceedingly changeable, and the summer of 1588 was particularly foul. Then, as now, far-sighted men had become alarmed by the rate at which the forests were being cut down for house- and ship-building. Already Kent was the garden of England, with many orchards and numerous warrens of rabbits kept for the London market.

Then, as now, the Government was battling to establish some sort of a balance in agriculture. In the middle of the century the prosperity of the cloth industry, and the strong demand for English wool, had led many farmers to put their land down to grass; so a series of Tillage Acts sought to increase the production of corn by placing penalties on those who went out of cultivation. Enormous anxiety was caused by the continual enclosure, or fencing-in by individuals, of land that had once been common, and available to all who lived round it.

Country people lived an extremely simple life, sleeping on bare boards and owning nothing beyond a few pots, pans and rudimentary furniture, most of which they had built themselves. Eating utensils — bowls, plates and spoons — were all made of wood, and carved at home.

Then, as now, the curse of the land was unemployment, and a bad harvest would leave thousands of peasants destitute; those without work were driven across country by hunger to look for better things, thus creating one of the worst headaches of Elizabethan England — vagrancy. The Government's most intractable social problem was to devise some system of poor relief.

An excellent contemporary witness for such matters is William Harrison — graduate of both Oxford and Cambridge, antiquarian, numismatist, keen gardener, household chaplain to Lord Cobham and sometime vicar of Wimbish, in Essex — who became Canon of Windsor in 1586, and a year later published his book *Elizabethan England.*

This divine had little sympathy for vagrants, and recorded unemotionally that although the punishment ordained for vagabonds was 'very sharp', yet 'it cannot restrain them from their gadding'. Anybody convicted was 'immediately adjudged to be grievously whipped and burned through the gristle of the right ear with a hot iron of the compass of an inch about'. A second offence called for similar treatment of the left ear, and a third for death.

After inveighing against 'counterfeit vagrants', who cultivated sores or maimed themselves to attract sympathy, Harrison listed the 'several disorders and degrees' among genuine vagabonds: '1. Rufflers. 2. Uprightmen.

3. Hookers or anglers. 4. Rogues. 5 Wild rogues. 6. Priggers or pransers. 7. Palliards. 8. Fraters. 9. Abrams. 10. Freshwater mariners or whipjacks. 11. Drummerers. 12. Drunken tinkers. 13. Swaddlers or pedlers. 14. Jarkemen or patricoes.'

Much as one longs to know the exact difference between a jarkeman and a pranser, it would be even better to have distinguishing features for those whom Harrison lists 'of the women kind': '1. Demanders for glimmer or fire. 2. Bawdy baskets. 3. Mortes. 4. Autem mortem. 5. Walking mortes. 6. Doxies. 7. Dells. 8. Kinching mortes. 9. Kinching cooes.'

Another subject close to Harrison's heart was beer, which his wife used to brew for him in batches of 200 gallons. In country ale houses, he wrote, 'there is such heady ale and beer as is commonly called "huffcap", "the mad dog", "Father Whoreson", "angels' food", "go by the wall", "stride wide" and "lift leg" etc.' He found it incredible to see 'how our maltbugs lug at this liquor, even as pigs lie in a row lugging at their dame's teats . . . till they be red as cocks and little wiser than their combs'.

Harrison's account of the countryside emphasises the huge numbers of sheep, which were easy to keep, for although wolves still flourished in the wilds of Wales and Scotland, they had been eliminated from England. 'Our sheep pass all other for sweetness of flesh,' he wrote, 'and so much are our wools to be preferred before those of Milesia and other places that if Jason had known the value of them that are bred and to be had in Britain, he would never have gone to Colchis to look for any there.'

Harrison was particularly anxious about the decline of the woods, and proposed a law that every man with forty or more acres of land should be compelled to plant one acre of trees — oak, hazel and beech — and make provision for it to be kept and cherished. He attributed the loss of forest cover largely to the new fashion for building. In the old days, he remarked, men used to be content with houses of 'sallow, willow, plum tree, hornbeam and elm'. Now they all wanted oak — and in this sudden demand for extra security he detected a lamentable moral and physical degeneracy:

'And yet see the change! For when our homes were built of willow, then we had oaken men; but now that our homes are come to be made of oak, our men

are not only become willow, but a great many, through Persian delicacy crept in among us, altogether of straw.'

To their descendants four centuries later, the Elizabethans do not seem like men of straw. Far from it: they seem exceedingly tough and cruel — and no doubt it is as well for us that they were, when the Spaniards came.

Arthur's Little Friends

Nowhere in the kingdom will you find a man closer to the earth than Arthur Hollins, who farms near Market Drayton in Shropshire. 'Look at that!' he says triumphantly as he pulls up the crust of a half-baked cowpat with both hands. 'There they all are — hard at it!'

'They' are his friends the worms and insects and other minute creatures which inhabit the top three or four inches of the ground. Attracted by juice percolating down from the fresh dung above, they have come up and eaten away the whole underside of the cowpat, thereby transferring essential nutrients through their bodies to the soil.

A small, slight man of seventy-six, with straggly white hair, Arthur looks hardly robust enough to be a farmer — and indeed in his youth he was such a weakling that a doctor once gave him a year to live. Yet he has devoted his whole long life to practical husbandry; he still works outdoors from dawn to dusk, and among connoisseurs of organic agriculture he has established a reputation as a wizard in the management of pastureland.

As tenants of a local landowner, his family have lived and worked at Fordhall Farm for generations; but Arthur was pitched into action prematurely, for his father died when he was only thirteen. The farm was then thoroughly run down: more than half its 150 acres were little better than a marsh, down by the river Tern, and the rest were thin soil which grew poor arable crops.

Arthur dedicated his life to cracking the farm's problems. His family were up to their ears in debt, but he managed to persuade their landlord to let them remain in possession, promising that he would one day pay back what they owed (he did, but it took him twenty-five years).

They all pitched in, changed from Shorthorns to Jerseys, went into milk and began to sell yoghurt, cottage cheese and clotted cream all over the country. Collecting manure from racing stables round about, they grew mushrooms everywhere: in the farm buildings, the cellar, even the back room. In 1945 Arthur married, and with his wife May later opened a restaurant. His longest single job has been to drain the low-lying meadows — a herculean task at last reaching completion.

Yet behind his day-to-day work there has always lain a tremendous thirst for knowledge. A born investigator, he was determined to find out why his land had lost its fertility, and for the past fifty years he has carried on a programme of continuous research.

His main discovery has been of the vital role which bacteria and other organisms play in the top few inches of the soil. Briefly, he found that animal manure is of limited value on its own, and that it is the consumption of it by worms and other far smaller organisms — the passage of it through their bodies, and the attack on it by the bacteria in their guts — which releases vital chemicals into the earth.

Everything depends on the condition of the precious top layer. Ideally, light must be excluded, so that bacteria can thrive, and the soil animals can eat away at the dead vegetable matter falling from above. Clearly, the plough is the worst possible enemy, for by breaking the ground open it destroys the intricate balance which nature has formed for itself. In Arthur's view, 'The plough unbuttons everything.'

Building on this knowledge, he put all his fields down to grass and evolved his present system of managing pastureland. For thirty years he has used no artificial fertilisers or chemical sprays. In all that time he has never made hay or silage. He does not bring his cattle in during the winter, or feed them (except sometimes with a bit of straw). And yet his grass looks wonderful, with a dense, springy sward containing numerous varieties of grass and herbs, and beneath it the soil has a perfect, crumbly texture.

His secret is to keep adjusting the intensity with which each field is grazed, so that different plants, which flower at different seasons, all get their chance to mature in turn. If some kinds of grass are allowed to grow up high, for instance, they suppress the clover, but when they are grazed down hard, the clover soon spreads again.

A continuous three-year rotation enables soil animals to flourish, and keeps building up the land's fertility without chemical help. Thus Arthur can run 120 head of beef cattle and 100 sheep on his 150 acres, and because his input is minimal, he makes a good living from the farm, selling pork, poultry and eggs as well. Since all his produce is organic, it commands a fifteen per cent premium, and he cannot satisfy demand. (Having tried his bacon, I am not surprised, for it has an intensity of flavour which takes me back to my childhood.)

Over the years various esoteric experiments have contributed to his knowledge. In one, he went to the length of staying up all night with a cowpat and watching what happened as it cooled. He found that at about seventy degrees it formed a crust which shut out the light, encouraging insects and bacteria to get busy underneath.

In another trial he fed stones to mature geese and turkeys. The birds were in cages, and with their normal food of grain and grass he gave them stones as big as his fingernail. They ate them all, but passed none through in their droppings, thereby demonstrating a bird's extraordinary power to dissolve rock.

This, says Arthur, is why poultry manure is the richest in nature: the bacteria in the birds' gizzards are able to convert stone back into the chemicals from which it was constituted millions of years ago. For this reason he welcomes wild birds as unpaid assistants.

In yet another trial, he scraped away all the plant life from under a large horse-chestnut tree and kept the ground bare. Gradually the soil went to sleep, until there was no activity in it, and no release of chemicals. The tree fell sick, and in the ninth year, on a still morning, it suddenly toppled over. Now, propped up on its branches, which embedded themselves in the ground as it fell, it lies in the garden like a huge sculpture, and an awesome testimony to plant power.

Arthur's theories have not made him universally popular. Organic gardeners, for instance, take umbrage when he tells them that to make compost is the worst thing they can do, since it produces bacteria used to living at such a high temperature that they are unfit for service in the ground.

Makers of agricultural machinery view with alarm his 'Pulvoseeder', a patent cultivator of which a prototype stands in one of his barns. This revolutionary device will, he hopes, render plough and harrow obsolete — and on Thursday he made a rare visit to London, to meet a group of MPs and others who may help finance its development.

The principle of the machine is that it disturbs the ground as little as possible, slicing off a two-inch layer, inserting seed, shaking earth back on to it and leaving a light-excluding carpet of trash on top. Arthur's dream is to produce models of various sizes, the smallest suitable for gardeners, the biggest a full-scale farming implement.

His other main hope is that his son will succeed him on the farm. After the tragic death of his first wife in a car accident, he married again, and now has a boy of seven. As he himself says, 'When you get past seventy, you start counting the years a bit'; nevertheless, he has every intention of staying around until young Ben is big enough to take over.

Stuck for an Answer

It has been mercifully rare, in my experience, to find that I cannot understand a single word of the conversation. If one arrived suddenly in the wilds of Japan or China, one would positively expect to be in the dark; but in Europe one generally reckons to pick up the odd word here and there.

Not so for much of an afternoon spent in the company of three Bavarian farmers. Charming men, they were extremely polite, and whenever they spoke to me made an effort to use proper German. In this mode two of them were tolerably comprehensible, but the third was an old man with no teeth who mumbled so thickly that I could decipher only about one word in ten. When they spoke to each other, they naturally lapsed into Bavarian, and might, as far as I was concerned, just as well have been talking ancient Etruscan.

I supposed that it would be much the same, the other way round, if a German found himself landed among farmers in Carmarthenshire. If they spoke to him in English, he would understand precious little because of their accents, and if they fell into Welsh, nothing at all.

In Bavaria, the main characteristic of the local accent is to add a soft e at the end of each word, as if turning it into a diminutive. Thus *Hase* (hare) sounds like *Harzi* instead of *Harza, Fasan* (pheasant) becomes *Fasane,* a badger *Dachs* is *Dachse* and so on. Even numerals are converted into *zwanske, dreiske, vierske,* as though the person were pretending to count in Russian.

Linguistically, then, it was a testing afternoon, but in other respects most rewarding, for as always I found it a delight to see fresh woods and pastures new. Like Britain, Bavaria had no winter to speak of, and everything except the freezing temperature was weeks ahead of schedule. My companions were fascinated when, on the edge of a wood, we found the tiny track of a badger-cub, sketched lightly in the mud behind the bigger prints of its mother. It was extraordinary, they said, that the little fellow could be on the move so soon.

One of their preoccupations was the disappearance of hares. Once they used to shoot 200 hares in a day. Now there are so few that, when we spotted one, it had to be studied at length through binoculars. There were mutterings about some mysterious virus, but no one really knew what has caused the decline.

The single hare we saw looked healthy enough, and as we watched it slowly lower its ears in response to our scrutiny, my mind went back to an earlier occasion in northern Germany, when some Coldstream guardsmen were impressed as beaters for a large-scale shoot. Up there in the Rhineland, accents are harder, and, far from adding syllables at the end of words, farmers drop aspirates and endings with abandon.

Thus, whenever a hare got up, its appearance was greeted with cries not of two syllables but of one. At first the guardsmen were unable to believe their ears and fell about laughing; but in a few minutes they too were shouting out 'Arse! Arse!' with the best of them.

Down in the south, the lone hare went loping off, and soon, as we drove along a grass track between fields of young wheat, we came to a limestone quarry. Through the mumble of my toothless neighbour I suddenly discerned the word '*Archaeopteryx*', and deciphered the core of his message: that the wonderful fossil which I had seen in the local museum that morning — one of only five in the world — had been found on this very spot.

Archaeopteryx was quite small — only a foot or so from head to tail — but an extraordinary link between reptile and primeval bird, with long legs, toothed beak (or jaws), three clawed fingers on each foot, and ribs instead of breastbone. It made my day to have seen the petrified environment of a creature so prodigiously old, and to think that perhaps fifty million years ago bony, leathery shapes flapped heavily over this high landscape.

After that, I did not feel particularly interested by a fine cock pheasant which appeared in a field and to my companions was a rarity as exciting as the hare; but somehow it no longer seemed to matter that I could not penetrate the ancient Etruscan burbling out beside me.

The experience made me reflect on how compressed many of our own bucolic expressions are, and how misleading they would be to a foreign visitor. For instance, the phrase 'very near time' would probably indicate to a stranger that something was about to happen in the immediate future. Little could he know that when somebody staggers out of the pub into the pitch-dark Gents and says, 'Very near time 'e 'ad a light put in 'ere', the speaker is expressing his conviction that the landlord should have installed electricity years ago.

Equally, a foreigner would have little chance of spotting that what sounds like 'sha-latter' is a corruption of 'we shall have to' — as in 'sha-latter get they gutters cleared out, shan't us?' When I come to think of it, I see that half my local conversations are carried on in this cryptic form of shorthand.

Even so, I devoutly hope that all such linguistic idiosyncrasies survive indefinitely, and that if, after 1992, the European Government starts issuing directives for the regularisation of rural language, they will be treated with the contempt they deserve.

May

Exit Agamemnon

It grieves me to report that our prize-winning Wiltshire Horn ram Agamemnon is dead. In the end he became so bad-tempered that we felt we had no option but to put him down.

The news will, I am sure, come as a blow to his fans, not least the lady in Norfolk who once declared him to be her 'favourite thug in the English language'. Earlier this year, when stories appeared in the press about a ram killing a farmer, several people wrote letters of warning, some addressed to me, others to Agamemnon himself: all contained friendly cautions about the risks of having malevolent sheep at large.

The advice was well-meant but superfluous, for ever since, in his youth, our fellow sent a man flying head-first over a fence, we had kept him out of fields with public footpaths running through them. We had no doubt that if he ever managed to get a human victim on the ground, one well-directed charge would crush his or her rib-cage like an egg-shell.

This meant, in effect, that he had to spend most of his time in one or other of two paddocks immediately above the house — a vantage point which unfortunately gave him a commanding view of the garden. Watching moodily from above, he would wait until someone came out of the house, loose off volleys of imperious bleats, and then, if that person did not feed him or pay him close attention, he would very soon resort to physical violence.

First he would beat up a clump of comfrey with his horns; next he would start butting a fence-post from close range and scraping his horns back and forth across the wire netting stapled to it. If that did not produce results, he would withdraw half a dozen steps, take one pace to the left, measure the distance to the nearest post, and put in a full-scale charge, leaping the last few feet in a single bound so that his frontal bone whacked into the base of the target. Such was his weight and impetus that at the very least the post would be knocked back in its socket; often, with a sharp crack, it would shatter or break, and the rails connecting it with its neighbours would snap or fly off.

After every assault, repairs were needed. The expense was considerable, the wear on our nerves much greater. At one stage we took the wrecked fence down altogether, rebuilding it with stronger posts and only a single wooden rail along the top, instead of the two which we had had before, in the hope that it would offer a less attractive target.

If anything, the change seemed to increase Agamemnon's resentment. One of us had only to appear in the garden for him to open hostilities, and in summer his particular *bête noire* (or, strictly speaking, *rouge*) seemed to be the mower. Hardly had I begun cutting when, above the roar of the engine, I would be tormented by the splintering crack that signalled the demise of expensive timber.

The more we tried to divine the reasons for his behaviour, the more certain we became that he was merely seeking to attract notice. He was evidently not trying to break out, for he never attempted to push down the sheep-netting between him and the next field. Nor was he trying to attack the mower, which he simply used as an excuse. What he wanted was our undivided attention.

If one of us went up to the fence, he would present himself broadside-on, as if saying, 'Surely you can see me?' — a trick also practised by male llamas. There he would stand, wagging his tail and licking his lips as one scratched his back. Yet the difference between acceptance and attack was perilously small: the moment one stopped scratching, he would square up to smash the fence, and if ever I climbed over into his field, he would instantly prepare to charge.

After every satisfying high-decibel impact on timber, he would stand looking round, exactly like a spoilt child, to see what reaction his latest outrage had provoked. The one thing which he could not bear was to be ignored.

The time of year at which he gave least trouble was the autumn, when he was with his ewes; and several people asked why we did not furnish him with company at other seasons as well. The answer was that from time to time we did, and the results were disastrous.

Long-term readers of this column may recall that he killed a rival ram, Rivet, after an apparent truce had suddenly turned into full-scale combat. At other times we gave him, as companions, some immense superannuated wethers (neutered males), but these he tended to treat as punch-bags, and we feared it would be only a matter of time before he killed them too.

Not the least of our difficulties was the fact that, maddening though he became, we were very fond of him: he had after all been born on the farm, and in earlier days had often behaved in endearingly ridiculous fashion. In some of his antics — high skips performed by an exceedingly stout party — there was a kind of heroic buffoonery.

Besides, we blamed ourselves for having contributed to his neuroses by making too much fuss of him when he was a lamb: by halter-breaking him so that we could take him to a show (where he won first prize of £8 and a cup), we made him altogether too familiar with humans. Most sheep instinctively give people a wide berth, but in him this natural defence mechanism had broken down.

All this weighed on our minds as we debated his future. At five years old, he was already past his prime. He had fathered numerous good lambs, and contributed strongly to the come-back which his breed is making; but we ourselves did not want any more of his genes, for fear of our stock becoming inbred. Had he been more amenable, he could have been honourably pensioned off, either at home or with friends; but as things were, he was far too unreliable to be sold or given away.

So at last we hardened our hearts and sent for the man from the local hunt, who expertly despatched him with a humane-killer and took his body away. One small consolation was that he knew nothing whatever about what happened. One moment he was getting the close attention he craved; the next, he was 250lb of meat.

Now we miss him. It is no small relief that I can mow, and my wife can weed the flower-beds, without peremptory roars and the crash of shattered wood constantly breaking out above us; all the same, his paddock seems empty, even when other animals are grazing it. I suppose that the disappearance of an outsize ego is bound to leave a gap.

'Vixere fortes ante Agamemnona' wrote Horace 2,000 years ago: there lived heroes before Agamemnon. What he meant, and went on to say, was that countless giants of yore had vanished without trace because they had had no poet to sing their praises.

Well — now I have sung our Agamemnon's praises here, and earlier, so perhaps he will not be forgotten. And in any case, there hangs in our porch a powerful likeness of him, done in oils by my sister-in-law, which catches to perfection the sweep of his horns and the baleful glare of his yellow eyes.

It did cross my mind to call in a taxidermist, and have his head and neck mounted — but the effect, I think, might have been rather overpowering. The portrait is·reminder enough. To all who enter, it gives pause. 'My God,' visitors say, looking up uneasily. 'Whatever's that?' And so I tell them, and for a while the great booby lives again.

Man with Swinging Rods

The advertisement in a specialist country magazine said, 'Roy Talbot, Dowser,' and I rang the number in Shropshire to explain that we were curious to know whether or not we had, beneath our land, any watercourses which could be tapped to create a small lake. The answer, in short, was that if I sent a large-scale map, or drew a plan, Talbot (for £30) would do a 'map-dowse', and we would soon find out.

'But how can you tell anything from a map?' I asked.

'It's hard to explain,' came the answer, 'but I can. My results are eighty-seven per cent correct — and if, in the end, you don't find water where I've marked it, I refund your fee.'

Hooked, I sent off a section of the twenty-five-inches-to-the-mile Ordnance Survey map. I marked the boundary of our land on it, but I noticed that the sheet bore no contours, so that it was impossible for anyone who did not know the place to discern which way the ground sloped.

In a few days, back came my map. To our amazement, Talbot had found not one but four aquifers running beneath our fields, designated A-A, B-B, C-C, D-D. Nor was that all: he had divined their size, depth, pressure and direction, and in a covering letter he suggested that B-B should prove the best of the bunch: 'Aquifer B-B indicates an easterly flow of somewhat less than 3,000 gallons per hour of potable water at medium pressure about eighty feet below ground level.'

By what seemed an extraordinary fluke, he had selected as the most advantageous place for a bore the precise spot on which we hope to have our lake. But had he not made an elementary mistake? He said that Aquifer B-B was flowing eastwards: that meant it was going up, or at any rate into, a one-in-four hill.

I was fascinated, and rather disturbed. It seemed uncanny that someone who had never been near our home could find out so much about it; and now, although the next stage — a site visit — would cost £150, plus travelling costs, I knew we had to go through with it.

Talbot turned out to be a calm, stocky man of fifty-eight, a freelance management consultant for two-thirds of his time, a dowser for the rest. Over coffee in the kitchen he told us that he had been dowsing for thirty years, and was still learning. 'Almost everyone can do it,' he said. 'I've taken sixty people at a village fete, and fifty-eight of them could dowse. It all depends on how you develop the skill.'

He told us of earlier jobs: how he had found the only water on the Greek island of Hydra; how he traced leaks for water boards; how he located old tunnels for construction engineers; how things sometimes went wrong — as when, near Banbury, he tried to pinpoint a soakaway but instead created an artesian water-spout.

At first our questions were blundering. 'What do you *see*?' I asked. 'Do you *feel* anything?' The answer to these was 'Nothing' and 'No' — and, for all his experience, Talbot found it easier to demonstrate than to explain.

For dowsing the map, his instrument was a home-made pendulum: a small, empty medicine bottle, with fine string threaded through the centre of the cap. With his left elbow propped on the kitchen table, he held the string between thumb and forefinger and let the pendulum dangle. With his other hand he moved a pencil over the map: as the tip reached a certain position, the bottle suddenly began going round, rather than back and forth, and from its responses he traced out the course of an underground stream.

As I understood it, he was asking the pendulum definite questions, to which the answer could only be 'Yes' or 'No': 'Is this electricity?' 'Is this natural?' 'It is flowing this way?' and so on. To find out the depth, he wrote out a column of figures, from 0 to 100, and checked down it with the pencil until, at 80, the pendulum began to go.

Many people would have been sceptical. We were not. Talbot was transparently honest and serious. Between calculations, he emphasised how anxious he was to dispel the image of the dowser as charlatan and magician. 'There's nothing magical about it,' he insisted. 'It's a purely mental exercise.'

In the field, his main instruments were a pair of rods made of fencing-wire bent at right angles. He was not in the least put out by the steep slopes. 'I'm interested in the strata down below,' he said, 'not in the surface of the earth. Contours have nothing to do with it.'

In the area he had marked B-B, he teed himself up like a rugger player about to take a place-kick, breathed deeply, with his eyes half closed in concentration, and began to walk slowly forward with the rods held out horizontally in front of him. Suddenly they swung violently apart. He put a small marker in the ground, went back and made another pass. This time the rods did not move. He stopped, turned, made a pass in the other direction. Again no movement. But on the fourth pass the rods swung again.

More pegs went into the ground, marking a line. Then he consulted his pendulum a few times, with his left hand held out, palm vertical, at arm's length. At last, unable to bear the suspense any longer, I asked what he had found.

'Oh', he said, as if surprised that I did not know. 'This is the stream. You have a stream running in a rock fissure under high pressure. It's flowing that way (towards the hill), at about 3,000 gallons per hour. It's about seventy feet down. The fissure is seven or eight feet wide. The stream won't be artesian, but it will rise to within about twenty feet of ground level in the bore . . .'

The row of pegs was within a yard or two of the line he had marked on the map. On the passes which proved negative, he had been asking, 'Is this electricity?' 'Is this man-made?'

Back in the kitchen, he began doing more calculations, and suddenly asked, 'Is it possible that this house was begun in September 1608?'

All I could say was that the date seemed right. After he had gone, I checked up with Neil Taylor, Managing Director of Tyrone Soil Engineering, a firm based at Bicester for whom Talbot had done several jobs, locating old tunnels and workings beneath land on which new building was planned.

Mr Taylor agreed that dowsing is often extremely useful. 'There's no question that it makes a definite contribution,' he said. 'We find Roy a great help, because, not having X-ray eyes, we can't find old swallow-holes, tunnels or cavities like he can.' At the same time, Taylor added that he had to be circumspect in writing reports, because many clients would react unfavourably 'if they found that, alongside scientific techniques, we had been using a system that's been with mankind since the year dot.'

Such a notion does not worry me. On the contrary, I find it exciting to have tuned in vicariously to the system of universal intelligence which seems to prevail, even though most humans have lost the ability to plug into it. All we need now is the money to pay for drilling. Roy Talbot's last words before he left were, 'I'll bet me trousers you find water down there' — and I'll bet mine he's right.

Prisoners in the Mansion

Trapped at sundown in a cavernous, decaying stone mansion, abandoned by its builders in 1868 and now inhabited only by bats . . . It sounds like the opening of a horror movie. So I would have thought — until it happened to me.

Together with Mike Hill, an architect expert in historic buildings, I had gone to make a survey of Woodchester Park, the unique Victorian-gothic house near Stroud, which, after many vicissitudes, is about to get a new lease of life. It belongs to the Stroud District Council, who bought it in 1987 to save it from collapse; but it is now being taken over by a body of local enthusiasts, the Woodchester Mansion Conservation Group, which plans to stabilise and preserve it as a centre for the training of stone-masons.

The mansion stands on its own, far down a deep, wooded valley, and at first sight creates a sinister impression. Stone gargoyles in the form of mythical beasts sprout horizontally from its main facade — in fact they are rainwater chutes — and little stone bats, owls and monkeys perch on the pointed gables of its roof. In recent years its remote position has made it a target for vandals, so that all the ground-floor windows are walled or boarded up to keep out intruders.

It was four o'clock on a sunny afternoon when we arrived. A young kestrel sat on a fence post by the front door, watching us fearlessly from a distance of five yards, while the rest of its family flew in and out of an upper window, giving their characteristic shrill cries.

After a brief tour of the outside, Mike undid two combination padlocks on the bolts that secured the makeshift door, and in we went, to record a description of the interior. The house is riveting, not least because it was left half-completed 120 years ago. Its hall-mark is stonework of the highest quality: door-frames, fireplaces and vaulted ceilings are all made of limestone beautifully carved and finished. In the south range most of the rooms have no ceilings, so that one can look straight up through three storeys some fifty feet to the roof.

The whole place has a strongly ecclesiastical feel, for its owner, William Leigh, was a convert to Roman Catholicism, and wanted to create a replica of a medieval monastic community. The finely-vaulted chapel, built into the eastern side of the house, is one of its glories.

After about an hour, as we moved slowly from room to room with a tape-recorder, compiling a guide for future visitors, I wanted to answer a call of nature and made for the front door . . . only to find that I could not move it. Pushing and shaking established that the lower of the two bolts on the outside had somehow settled into its slot in the concrete sill.

We thought for a moment that some joker had come along and shut us in. Then we decided that the bolt must simply have slipped. Either way we were — as Conan Doyle might have put it — in Queer Street.

Along the foot of the door was a gap about half an inch high. By putting the sides of our heads on the floor, we could see the bolt through it, but it was too narrow for fingers to pass underneath. Mike began to probe and fiddle, trying to raise the bolt with a sliver of wood. That seemed hopeless to me, and I said, 'Surely it's easy enough to climb out of a window?'

'I don't think you'll find it is,' he said evenly. Leaving him on his knees, I set off along the main corridor, up the stone stairs and over the unfinished vaults of the drawing-room ceiling. The prospect from the unglazed window was not reassuring. So huge is the house, so grand its conception, that even from the first floor there is a drop of about twenty-five feet into stone vaults choked with nettles.

No good. Hurrying a bit, I set off for the back of the building, which stands tight against the hill. It would be an exaggeration to say that the light was fading

— it was still only five o'clock — or that my footsteps rang through the stone corridors, for I was wearing trainers. All the same, I did not feel entirely at ease.

There was no food in the building, of course, and no water. We had no extra clothes, nor any means of communicating with the outside world. But people knew where we had gone, and if we did not return to our homes by nightfall, they would surely come looking . . .

It so happened that, as part of my research, I had just read various stories about Woodchester. One concerned the second Earl of Ducie, who owned a Georgian house on this site. A bit of a rake, he celebrated his succession to the title by throwing a grand dinner party, at which he seated his lady of the moment in the place of honour, only to find his own chair occupied by the ghost of his recently-expired father. The shock is said to have been so great that it drove him headlong from the house, which he sold to William Leigh.

Other tales described how a centurion is inclined to pass up and down near the gates on the south road, and how 'a reprehensible Earl' is sometimes seen riding along the drive. A dwarf in rags, a headless horseman and a floating, coffin-shaped object are all alleged to frequent this secret valley.

All this rose easily to the surface of my mind as I ranged from room to room. Everywhere the story was the same: at ground level the anti-vandal defences were immovable, and from higher up the drops would have been suicidal. Huge as it is, the building contained no rope or wire, still less any sheets that we could knot together.

Down in the hall, I joined Mike in his dogged battle. Having found a piece of rusty angle-iron, I began to chip away at the concrete below the door, using a lump of stone as a hammer and hoping to enlarge the gap enough for us to fiddle our fingers through.

Time passed. My thoughts would not stay on the job. They flitted from the first Earl of Ducie, returning like Banquo to the feast, to speculation of about where, if we were forced to spend the night, it would be least uncomfortable to pitch up.

I decided that I should certainly avoid the chapel — the spookiest room of all. Another area of which I should steer clear was the brewery, now the main stronghold of the bats. Perhaps the vast stone bath, carved from a single block, would make a reasonable resting-place . . . Yet that too had a drawback, in that it is thought by certain paranormal groups to have been designed as the centrepiece of curious rituals which Leigh planned to practise behind the front of his Roman Catholicism.

Suddenly there came a breakthrough. Noticing that there was a little vertical movement in the door, I shoved my angle-iron under it and managed to lever it upwards nearly an inch. This gave Mike the clearance he needed: in a few seconds he had the bolt up, and we were free.

Outside, the sun was still hot; the kestrels were still screeching about their business. Everything looked reassuringly normal. Macabre Transylvanian fantasies evaporated into the balmy evening air.

If the truth be told, the better one gets to know the Mansion, the less sinister it becomes. It is an extraordinary house by any standards, but it has a friendly feel; and for those faced with the task of raising £3 million to save it, this is just as well.

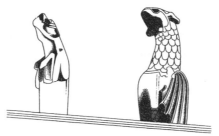

A Squire and his Trees

What could be more agreeable than to walk through summer woods in the company of an owner wholeheartedly devoted to their welfare?

Sir Marcus Worsley is lucky enough to have more than 700 acres of forest on the Hovingham estate, north of York; but he does not take his good fortune for granted. Far from it: he cherishes his woods, cares passionately about them, and manages them with the close attention that lesser landowners might lavish on their gardens.

On a recent visit, during which he showed me round, he began talking trees even before we reached the main block of woodland, which crowns a 400-foot hill. 'Those big limes mark the line of a 1740 canal,' he said as we set off in a jeep through what used to be a formal park. 'Roughly where that big ash stands, there was a Roman villa . . . In the eighteenth century these terraces were planted up with Scots pine . . . Those yews are really most inappropriate. They break the continuity, and we ought to take them out.'

Together with his son William, who helps run the 3,000-acre estate, he is in the middle of a major scheme for restoring the park's old clumps with a mixture of Scots pine and beech. Yet it is in the big woods on the hill that his heart really lies.

Their present state of excellence derives at least in part from the initiative taken by his grandfather, who succeeded to the baronetcy in 1897. Though not himself a great forester, the third Sir William Worsley took a close interest, and appointed as agent a young man of eighteen called Bingley Day who was passionately keen on trees. The result was a renaissance of woods which had already been cultivated for at least three centuries.

Continuity is the essence of the operation at Hovingham. Day remained agent for fifty-five years, and the present forester, Alec Brown, is from the third generation of his family to hold the job.

Another link with the past is the practice of using a horse for extracting small timber. The present horse is Duke; his predecessor was Prince. The estate may, as its owner remarks, be 'moving down market' in equine terms, but the animal is by no means a gimmick: on the contrary, he more than earns his keep. For one thing, he needs no road-tax, and can walk to work; more important, when a plantation is first thinned, he can move about in it without every fourth row of trees having to be sacrificed, as it must be to let in a tractor.

The beauty of the Hovingham woods lies largely in the fact that they are a mixture of broadleaved and evergreen species. Once mostly oak, they now include sycamore, ash, beech, sweet chestnut and alder, along with larch, Scots and Corsican pine, Norway spruce, and West American species such as Douglas fir, Sitka spruce and Tsuga, or Western Hemlock. There is also a good deal of cherry — the result of an ancestor's addiction to the poems of A.E. Housman.

Indeed, one of the owner's cardinal beliefs is that mixed woods are by far the most handsome. 'Monoculture of *any* species looks dull,' he says — and he points out with relish that his forebears planted conifers in the eighteenth century 'because they were bored stiff with miles of solid hardwood.'

He even enters into vigorous defence of sitka, a species execrated because it has been planted in million-strong blankets over moor and mountain. As he can readily demonstrate by exhibiting full-grown specimens, if given a chance, sitka reach magnificent dimensions.

Soon after Sir Marcus got married, he told his wife that if ever she were asked her opinion about a particular plantation, all she need do, to establish a reputation for silvicultural wizardry, was to look the trees over and say, 'They need thinning'. The odds were that she would be right — and vigorous thinning remains a key element of policy, with the result that most of the woods have an attractively open texture.

Moving round his rides, Sir Marcus demonstrates impressive knowledge of every plot. 'This is P.48,' he announces without recourse to any notes (meaning that the block was planted in 1948 . . .). 'This is P.41'

If you simply look at a wood from the outside, he says, 'you think you know what's going on inside — but in fact you don't.' It is therefore a firm rule that, once every two years, he, William and the forester together walk through every plantation, making notes on a tape-recorder and writing a short report. His aim, now, is to file these biennial comments on a computer, so that retrospective checks will become simple.

Vexations abound. One is that the land seems incapable of growing good beech. Instead of going up smooth and straight, beech trunks twist and corrugate. Thinking that there must be something wrong with the local strain, Sir Marcus imported seed from impeccably straight parents — only to find that the trees which grew from them twisted as badly as their predecessors.

Other problems include roe deer, which nip the leading shoot out of saplings and fray bark with their antlers. The gamekeeper wages intermittent war on them, and continuous war on grey squirrels, which are highly destructive. But the most ubiquitous enemy of new plantations is grass.

'People think grass is harmless,' says Sir Marcus testily. 'But it's absolutely NOT harmless. It gives young trees the most horrible competition.' To keep it at bay, he gets his forester to spray round each sapling with herbicide in early summer, creating a circle of clear earth at least a yard across, and so allowing the tree the maximum moisture and nutrients.

Perhaps the most impressive feature of forestry at Hovingham is that, even if it gives so much aesthetic satisfaction, it is essentially a commercial operation. The aim is that it should make money — and it does. As soon as a stand of timber is mature, it is clear-felled and the ground is replanted. The programme for felling is already worked out until the year 2020.

Occasionally the owner has a pang. 'Look at that sitka. Fifty years old. It should be in my bank statement. But isn't it splendid!' For the most part, though, he is entirely practical; 'This lot are worth £10,000 a hectare. That's quite a bit of money to have standing up and not appreciating much. They've got to go.'

It was his father who began the policy, still continued, of naming woods after children born during the year of planting. Thus it would be ungallant to inquire too closely about the date of Katharine's Plantation — a mixture of larch, Douglas fir and sitka which marked the birth of his sister, the Duchess of Kent, but which reached its prime and was felled a year ago.

Another awkward problem is posed by Marcus's Plantation, now fast approaching maturity. 'This is a matter of some delicacy,' says its namesake, 'but it will have to come down, probably in '96.'

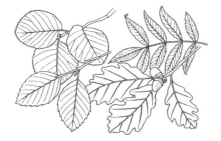

The great thing about this forester is that he does not *mind* felling trees. He sees felling and replanting, death and life, as part of the rhythm of nature, and himself draws strength from the unending process.

If ever he gets in a fuss about something, he finds that to walk through a wood is the best possible therapy. 'Trees seem to me to be great educators,' he says, 'because they have their own long-term way of looking at things. It's extraordinary what you can learn from them.'

Stallions on the Steppes

I hope it will not seem immodest if I say something about the background of my novel *Horses of War,* which was published this week. Whether or not the book is any good, it remains for others to decide; but the genesis of the story was unusual.

The gem of the idea came from a single paragraph in *The Bloodstock Breeders' Review* for 1938 — the annual summary of events on the turf. This riveting compendium — printed, like *Hansard,* with two columns on each page — included the substance of an interview given to the London *Evening Standard* by Joseph Clements, a former jockey who had gone out to Russia in 1895 and ridden successfully in races there. By 1938 he was back in England, and in 'a Newmarket infirmary'.

He said that in 1919, when the Russian civil war was at its height, and 'after a number of brood mares, yearlings and foals had been shot' by the Bolsheviks, he decided to save as many horses as he could. But because he was unable to get a special train, he set off on foot with only two stallions, heading south for the Black Sea, where the White Russian forces were still being bolstered by British military support. The horses he chose were Minoru and Aboyeur, both winners of the Epsom Derby.

Eventually, after a nightmare journey, he reached the sea, got the stallions on board a ship, and evacuated them to Constantinople; but there some White Russian officers, whom he had known before the Revolution in St Petersburg, said that they had 'more right' to the horses than he had, and took them over. Clements never saw them again.

Recourse to the *Evening Standard* of 19 November 1938 filled out the picture slightly. Clements was described as 'a little old man with a shock of grey hair and deep-set eyes'. He told the reporter that during the Revolution the value of his life savings of £30,000 (perhaps £600,000 in today's values) had been swept away 'in less than half a day', and that he started his trek from Kharkov, a city in the Ukraine 500 miles south of Moscow, where he held an appointment at the Imperial Stud Farm.

Wanting to build his story into a novel, and needing more background, I first tried to discover if anyone in England remembered Clements, or if any of his family survived. I knew he had been apprenticed in Newmarket; and since he had also been in hospital there at the end of his life, it seemed sensible to place a notice asking for information in local newspapers.

This turned up a Mr Bernard Clements, who, though no relation, made sensible suggestions for further inquiries. No descendant or relative of Joseph came forward, however. I myself began to haunt Newmarket — to prowl about the Heath, to frequent pubs which flourished in Clements' day, and to watch the strings of horses out at exercise. Luckily I had once driven a car to Kharkov and beyond, so that I had an idea of what the Ukraine looked like; but I engaged a lively Russian student to look up sporting records in Moscow.

In Newmarket, everyone was helpfulness personified. The Thoroughbred Breeders' Association kindly let me loose in their library (even though I at once broke their photocopier), and I gleaned a certain amount about racing in Tsarist Russia from their records.

At Lordship and Egerton Stud, out on the London Road, where Minoru had stood as a stallion after his Derby triumph, a lady gave up her afternoon to take me round the tree-lined gallops laid out by the royal trainer Richard Marsh at the turn of the century; and at the National Stud the Assistant Manager, Jonathan Grimwade, concentrated my mind no end by showing me a magnificent stallion called Roussillon, valued at £5.5 million.

Suddenly I felt I was on a hot scent, for at the National Stud a posse of grooms advanced the news that a family called Clements was still active in racing, up in Yorkshire. 'Stallion men, too,' said one of my informants. 'That's your lot, for sure.'

I wrote at once, explaining what I was up to; but answer came there none, so again I drew blank. Meanwhile, my assistant in Moscow was doing the same. I had passed on to her Clements's claim that he had twice won the 'Russian Derby', but she had not been able to find a trace of any such victories.

I began to wonder whether the old man in the infirmary had been shooting a line. The stallions Minoru and Aboyeur had certainly gone to Russia. They were famous animals — Minoru because he had won the Derby of 1909 carrying the colours of King Edward VII, and Aboyeur because he had won by default in 1913, at 100-1, after the suffragette Emily Davison had thrown herself in front of the King's horse at Tattenham Corner and brought it down.

After the Bolshevik revolution neither animal was heard of again — at least not in England. Odd rumours came back that they had been smuggled away to Serbia — part of Yugoslavia — but nothing definite was ever established.

Had Clements exaggerated, or even invented the whole exploit? Suddenly I found something which confirmed at least part of his story. On 19 November 1938 General Sir Tom Bridges, the distinguished cavalry officer, had given a radio talk describing famous horses he had met during his career.

Among them were my two. Sure enough, the general recalled how in March 1920, as officer in charge of embarkation at the port of Novorossisk, on the east coast of the Black Sea, he had suddenly found himself confronted by 'what seemed to be a little Russian soldier, who touched his cap smartly in Newmarket style and said, "Beg pardon, Sir. Got any room for me 'orses'?"

Now I saw what had happened in 1938. The *Evening Standard* had picked up the general's reminiscence, and tracked down the former jockey in Newmarket a couple of days later. But still I was not sure about Clements's career in Russia.

Then came another breakthrough. In Moscow Masha, now reinforced by her mother, braved the rats and floods of the Lenin Central Library yet again to turn up the vital information that Clements had twice won the *Warsaw* Derby (Warsaw was then part of Tsarist Russia). Although the biggest race in the calendar was the All-Russia Derby held in Moscow, the Warsaw Derby was the second most important event of the year. As details of Clements' career emerged from ancient magazines, I saw that he had indeed done as well as he claimed.

So the foundations of the story were secure. The only trouble was that I still knew practically nothing about the man himself. In spite of persistent efforts, I never found out what he did after his return to England. Did he have brothers, sisters or any other close relations? Did he marry? Did he father any children during his twenty-odd years in Russia?

Although so much remained obscure, there were certain facts of which I felt absolutely confident: that he was a good, tough man, of exceptional courage, and that he pulled off an amazing feat. To coax two highly-bred horses some 700 miles through the chaos of civil war, and in the depths of the Russian winter, was an heroic achievement.

In seeking to recreate his life, I therefore felt that I must do my best for him, and I hope that, even if details are wrong, I have done justice to a bold spirit.

Publication of the novel threw up the fact that Clements married while in Russia and had a son.

June

Out with the Rat Lady

Frail as a ghost, and almost as transparent, the old lady met us at her door. '*He isn't dead,*' she announced in a voice heavy with dread. 'I heard him running at half-past four yesterday.'

'Don't worry, dear,' said Jean Price, the redoubtable Senior Pest Officer for Stroud District Council. 'I never thought I'd get him first time but we'll do everything we can.'

This seemed an odd place for a squirrel: an estate of chalet-bungalows some way from any wood. But there, on the steep banks of lawn between the houses, stood the answer to the riddle: a couple of walnut trees, spared by the builders. Last summer's heavy crop of nuts had attracted the animal into the area.

Moments later we squeezed through a slot into the loft and began creeping about, knees uncomfortably balanced on the joists. Sure enough, there he was: with a sudden scurry, he hurtled along under the eaves, immediately below us, but out of sight. And sure enough, he had not eaten the bait of rat-poison which Jean had left on her first visit: scattered walnut shells showed that he had his own stores.

'We'll have to try something else,' she said. She produced a plastic bottle of turquoise tracking powder which she puffed out liberally over the floor in one corner — her hope being that the squirrel would run through it and, when it groomed itself, ingest the poison.

That was all she could do for the moment, so we eased ourselves back on to the landing and closed the door. The old lady, too frail to climb the stairs, was hovering below. 'It can't come down, can it?' she quavered, and we reassured her that no such invasion was possible; but her anxiety was painful to behold.

As we drove away, Jean pointed out that although the council has an obligation to deal with rats, mice and fleas — the three types of vermin which constitute health hazards — it does not have to tackle squirrels. Even so, squirrels chew the insulation of electric wires, 'and if the old lady went up in flames, we'd all feel very sorry'.

If we lived a few miles further west, in Wales, Jean would certainly be called Miss Price the Pest. Here she is variously known as the Rat Lady, the Mouse Lady, the Flea Lady or the Wasp Lady, depending on what sort of assistance she has rendered. But a day spent in her company left no doubt that she is a pillar of the community, as warmly welcomed as other members of the council are execrated. Everywhere in the steep valleys round Stroud people greeted her ebulliently.

Daughter of a local farmer, she has been in pest-control for fifteen years, having done spells in the army (as a telephonist), as a civilian telephonist, on a farm and in public relations. Middle-aged, compact, silver of hair and ruddy of cheek, she goes — and talks — like a whirlwind.

During the six hours I spent with her, she scarcely stopped moving or drew breath; and yet she combined this formidable energy with rare compassion, both for human beings plagued by vermin, and for the vermin itself. 'I don't like killing anything,' she said. 'After all, a rat doesn't know that it's being a nuisance.'

Our day began in her preparation room, a small arsenal of weapons and equipment. Two colleagues were loading doses of wheat laced with anti-coagulant poison into plastic food bags — easy to carry, and easy to lob into inaccessible nooks and crannies. Round the walls were shelves of other poisons, insecticides, mechanical traps and boxes of Hoy Hoy Trap-a-Roach cockroach catchers — effective devices made of cardboard, which fold up into tiny houses and detain customers on their sticky floors as the insects advance on strips of bait.

Pest control has its own calendar. Early spring and mid-autumn are the sewer seasons, when, with the help of the two-man sewer team, who lift the manholes, Jean turns her attention underground. Summer is wasp time; each of the three pest officers deals with about 200 nests a year. In autumn and winter rats draw into buildings — not just old houses, but modern ones as well. Whatever the target, Jean does not use acute, persistent poisons like strychnine or zinc phosphide.

Our first call was on a woman who thought her house was infested with poultry lice. In fact her problem was fleas: Jean knew this, as a specimen had been caught and sent in for examination. But as she deftly sprayed Crackdown insecticide — water-based and biodegradable — round the edges of every room, she was diplomacy itself, soothing the house-holder's worries with gentle assurances.

Back in the car, she confided that she preferred specimens sent in folded in Sellotape. 'We've had live bed-bugs scooped up into match-boxes. When you open the box, the damned things come out like hell in the night because they're so hungry.

'The other day we had to deal with body lice. There's this group of elderly men who look after themselves: they were absolutely crawling. Bit of a shock for young Pauline, my new assistant: we pulled back the bed-clothes, and there were these little old men with not a stitch on. We had to do the jolly lot — bath them, clear out the bedding, have a big bonfire . . .'

Our next call was also for fleas, apparently introduced by the ginger cat into a spick-and-span new house. As she sprayed, Jean kept up a commentary: 'I'm concentrating on the edges of the rooms, because everything runs round the edges. They're not going to lay their next generation in the middle, where you walk. They're survivors, too, aren't they?'

In this house, two of the family are being bitten, two not. That figures. 'It's something to do with skin texture,' says Jean. 'Take me. I must be a rotten host. I've had fleas jumping all over my trousers, but I've never taken one home with me. If the right person walks in the door, though, the larvae come to life, just like that.'

Away we went, to yet another flea-ridden house. This time the owner — an elderly man — had killed one of the blighters, and proudly handed over the corpse. Then came four rat-calls in succession, three of them at pubs.

The squalor in and around these establishments was beyond description. In the store-room of one, the floor round the deep-freezes and boxes of crisps and chocolate was thickly scattered with rat droppings. Outside, another rat had invaded the garden, which is open to the public, burrowing into a heap of earth and rubbish.

In both places Jean put down a judicious bombardment of poison, but passed no censure. Nor, of course, did I — but I felt outraged by the idleness of the landlords. How could they bear to live in such sleaziness?

It was a relief to call on the squirrel lady, whose house was clean and tidy; and the final problem of the day — rats under a chicken shed at the bottom of a garden — was out in the country and therefore seemed more natural. At 4.30 Jean was still talking flat-out — about how she goes in for bobbin-lace, how she breeds Manchester terriers, how she feeds her goats garlic and honey, how she once got stung eight times at a single wasps' nest.

She is some goer, this latter-day pied piper. I came away with the feeling that in every working day she does a tremendous amount of good — and it can only be a tribute to her efficiency that the letters on the number-plate of her van spell out the word DEAD.

In Merlin Country

Nearly a thousand feet below us the river Pysgotwr wound lazily between the rocks of its dramatic gorge. Low down, a pair of kestrels circled above a ravine, and in a cliff-face we could see a raven's nest, from which this year's young had already flown.

But most of our attention was focussed out beyond the river, on the hills of Central Wales which rolled away green and empty to the horizon, for somewhere above them a male merlin was hunting.

Once again Steve Parr, a freelance ornithologist now working jointly for the Forestry Commission and the Royal Society for the Protection of Birds, swung his hand-held aerial slowly back and forth, searching for a signal from the tiny radio lashed with fuse-wire to one of the bird's tail feathers.

'There he is!' he said. 'Moving from left to right. Now he's stopped. I reckon he's perched up somewhere.'

Behind us in the sitka spruce plantation his mate was brooding her clutch of three chicks on an old crow's nest near the top of a tree. We had already wrestled our way up through the spiky branches to check them — a huddle of grey and yellow down — and Steve had pronounced them in excellent order, growing strongly at the tender age of twelve days.

Now we were expecting the male to come back with whatever prey he had caught, and yield it up to the female in a ritual food-pass. She, then, would pluck the bird and take it to her young.

Along a ride just inside the plantation, patches of feathers dotted about a mossy bank showed where the female had been plucking, and bore witness to the industry of the hunter. Meadow pipits were easily his most common victims, and Steve reckoned that to keep his family going he would need to catch at least fifteen a day.

Out on the sunny hillside, as we waited, we discussed this most stylish of all British hawks. Sometimes known as the sparrowhawk of the uplands, the merlin favours altitudes between 800 and 1800 feet. The male is scarcely bigger than a blackbird, and in flight looks rather like a cuckoo, though with a shorter tail. His back is a fine slatey blue, his underparts barred buff and brown. Head on, his profile is so slim as to be almost invisible: like a Stealth fighter, he is scarcely detectable as he powers in towards a target.

Four or five years ago, ornithologists feared that the merlin had gone into a serious decline in Wales. Old nest sites on the ground, in heather or molinia grass, were being deserted, and the birds themselves seemed to be disappearing.

The reason for their demise — people claimed — was the spread of new plantations in the mountains. It was said that by putting huge blocks of hillside under trees, foresters had drastically reduced the area of open land on which merlins depend for food. Forestry, in other words, was the *bête noire* of the uplands, the destroyer of wildlife.

Recent research has largely disproved these claims. The current research project in particular has shown that, far from disappearing, the merlins have merely shifted their nest-sites into the new trees.

Steve Parr reckons that there are now about ninety breeding pairs in Wales. The twenty nests which he found last year produced an average of two and a half young apiece — a good performance. This year's average will be lower, as a result of the relentlessly wet weather in June, which made hunting difficult and may also have drowned some chicks. Even so, he reckons that the merlins are doing well.

So, indeed, are all the Welsh raptors. In the past two years the celebrated red kites had their best-ever breeding seasons, and peregrines have increased from the low point of the 1960s to their highest recorded total of some 260 breeding pairs.

The aim of this summer's survey is to find out more about the merlin's habits, especially the way it hunts. Impressions gained so far are that the male has several favourite areas which he works in turn. Having made three or four kills in one, he seems to try another for a while.

To capture the particular birds which he is studying, Steve set a mist net across a ride near the nest, put a stuffed tawny owl up on a dead tree, and played an owl call through a tape-recorder. The female, hurtling out to drive the intruder off her patch, was caught first time and fitted with a radio; soon afterwards the male came in with a pipit and was also netted.

Now, by switching to the female's frequency — 259 — Steve could pick up a stream of loud bleeps which showed that she was on or near the nest close behind us. By turning to 279, he could faintly hear another merlin, known as the Dalarwen male, far off on a different territory to the east. But the fellow we wanted was on 309, and should be somewhere much closer.

'I've got him!' Steve announced suddenly. 'He's heading towards us. Over the bluff there. He's coming in fast.'

The strength of the signal increased rapidly. Any moment, we should see him ... and there he was — a slim, fast, dark shape speeding with long wing-beats towards the trees.

From over the wood behind us came his shrill, whickering call. Immediately the female answered with loud cries of *kew, kew, kew, kew*. A food pass had been made, and was over in a flash. Already the female would be plucking, the male heading out on anther sortie.

As we slipped quietly away, my heart went out to those fine, bold birds and their strange ritual. I envy them the high and wild environment in which they live, and hope for their sake that man does nothing to wreck it.

★   ★   ★

Poachers often turn gamekeeper, but not many gamekeepers turn artist. One who did was Geoffrey Dashwood, the sculptor, whose wonderful bronze birds go on show to the public for ten days from tomorrow in a major retrospective exhibition at the Nature in Art gallery at Wallsworth Hall, north of Gloucester.

A thoroughly rebellious boy, Dashwood was always first in art at school. At fifteen he left and enrolled in the art college in Southampton, but hated it so much that he quit only five weeks later.

After a series of dead-end jobs, he was taken on by the Forestry Commission, and for five years worked as a ranger, culling deer in the New Forest. Then he set himself up as a freelance artist; he began sculpting ten years ago, and since then has gone from strength to strength.

The figures of birds which he creates are life-sized, and somehow catch the character of their subjects to an uncanny degree. He makes his models from plaster and synthetic clay, and tends to carve and pare them down, rather than build them up. The bronze casts are made in a foundry which now understands his requirements so well that it can reproduce exactly the finish and patina which he specifies without him having to supervise the operation.

Dashwood's birds have a hypnotic smoothness, but at the same time are fully alive, and radiate the qualities which he discerns in the original. His magpie is thus 'a bird of false bravado and loutish showmanship', his cockerel a 'symbol of masculinity or pompous chauvinism', his little owl 'a little wicked and rather comical'.

All are highly covetable, the only snag being that the price of even the smallest (a wren) is in four figures. And what, by chance, should his latest creation be, delivered to the foundry on Wednesday? A merlin.

Gorilla on the Green

Ever since we came to Gloucestershire, more than two years ago, I have been hearing rumours about the gorilla which used to live in the Cotswold village of Uley; but only in the past few days have I managed to obtain a coherent account of him.

His name was John Daniel (Johnny for short) and belonged to Miss Alyse Cunningham, who bought him at Ponting's department store as a baby. Although she normally lived in Knightsbridge, early in 1920 she rented a ramshackle cottage on the village green and installed her charge there — much to the initial alarm of the postman, who was startled out of his wits when the door was opened by a hairy, black stranger.

Johnny was way ahead of his time, for captive gorillas were then extremely rare. His exceptional affinity with humans was said to derive from the fact that he had been reared at the breast of a native woman. Whether or not this was true, he associated with people so eagerly, and (if one may use the term) aped human customs so enthusiastically, that his fame soon spread.

He had his own bedroom, slept in a bed between sheets and ate at table with a knife and fork. By no means abstemious, he developed a taste for kippered herrings, chocolate, port, sherry and brandy. He was, however, acutely sensitive to ridicule, and once covered his face in shame when somebody laughed at his choice of cutlery.

He had no difficulty in learning to open and shut the latch of the garden gate, or to work the pump on the green that still supplied householders with water. When taken for a walk, he usually wore a collar and lead; but for much of the time his owner allowed him to run free so that he could play hide-and-seek and rounders with the children who lived at the top end of the village.

He was then three years old, or the equivalent of five or six in human terms. When he did go for a walk, he shook hands with passers-by, and expected them to return his salutation. He would also escort his playmates to school, holding hands, and then go home on his own.

No one remembers him better than Reg Beeston, now eighty-three, who was fifteen that famous summer. The gorilla would jump on his shoulders for a ride, and was heavy enough to be a serious burden. He had quite a temper, too, if thwarted: once, as they were playing rounders, a boy deliberately tripped him up   whereupon he chattered with rage, seized one of the heavy stones that marked the edges of the green, and flung it down in front of him.

In those days Reg's father had a cobbler's business next to the pub, on the other side of the green from where the gorilla lived. To this friendly workshop Johnny would often repair, letting himself in uninvited and imitating the cobbler's actions with rasp or hammer — until he hit himself on the thumb, whereupon he would go bounding for home. Another of his favourite destinations stood a few doors down Fiery Lane, where he soon learned to operate the tap and refresh himself in old Conk Mills's cider shed.

His strength grew rapidly throughout the summer, but he never hurt any of the children, who all loved him. Only when he became over-excited, and began to drum on his chest or bounce up and down, did he have to be taken home to cool off.

A film of him in action included sequences of him washing with a sponge, having a tea-party and grappling — in the end successfully — with a soda-water syphon. This movie fascinated the audience when it was shown at a scientific (*sic*) meeting of the London Zoological Society, but it may also have led to Johnny's downfall, for it attracted the attention of American showmen.

Either because he was growing so large, or simply because she scented a commercial opportunity, his owner sold him to Ringling & Barnum's Circus in New York for 1,000 guineas. At the beginning of March he spent ten days at her house in London, getting to know the circus's representative, John T. Benson, who shared his bedroom, described him as 'the world's most wonderful animal', and announced that he had cost as much as three elephants. Johnny does not seem to have been much impressed by this eulogy, for at one stage he put in a savage attack on his new minder.

In spite of this *faux pas,* he sailed from London in style on 10 March 1921 aboard the steamer *Old North State,* in a specially made cabin constructed from a portable bungalow which had been furnished with a brass-railed bed, table, mirror and armchair. He took with him peaches, apricots, chocolate, brandy and port.

I am sorry to say that he was preceded across the Atlantic by another representative of Ringling & Barnum, who specialised in the collection of freaks, and took passage on the SS *Olympic* a day earlier with two German giants, a giantess aged twenty-five, three fat brothers (one of whom weighed over 600lbs), a midget and a man who could swivel his head through 180 degrees. Johnny, I feel confident, proved a more dignified passenger than any of these.

He seems to have stood the voyage well; but in New York he at once began to pine inconsolably. Minder Benson could not get through to him. Doctors found nothing wrong but decided that he was wasting away because he felt himself friendless and alone. The only thing which might save him, they thought, was the presence of Miss Cunningham; so they cabled her, and she hastily took ship for America. But when her liner was only one day out from Southampton, he expired. 'GORILLA DIES OF BROKEN HEART', cried the newspaper headlines.

Today, had she taken Concorde, Miss Cunningham might have reached her protégé in time to save him; but I cannot help feeling that she brought the disaster upon herself by her heartlessness in selling an animal which so depended on her.

The whole episode serves as a salutary reminder of how far our attitudes to animals have advanced in sixty-odd years. Anyone who sees the tribal groups of gorillas breeding contentedly in zoos such as Jersey or Howletts will shudder at the thought of a single animal cut off from his kind — even if he did have one halcyon summer in the Cotswolds.

John Daniel Lives Again

If I report that we recently spent most of one morning trying to persuade a chimpanzee to sit on the child's seat of our outdoor privy, alongside a middle-aged lady wearing a purple cloche hat, you may think I am pulling your leg. If I add that the chimp was called Jasper, and was disguised as a gorilla, you may further doubt my veracity.

Perhaps I had better explain. Last year I published an account of how a young gorilla known as John Daniel spent the summer of 1920 in the Gloucestershire village of Uley. He belonged to an eccentric lady called Alyse Cunningham who taught him to shake hands, sleep in a bed, eat with knife and fork, use a lavatory and so on. A remarkable animal by any standards, he is still remembered affectionately by a few old-timers who, as children, played with him on the village green.

My article caught the eye of a BBC producer, Nigel Finch, who is now making a half-hour documentary of John Daniel's life for *Arena,* to be broadcast on 16 December. Hence the unusual activity in our area, and hence in particular the concentration on our privy, which commended itself to the BBC researchers as the perfect setting for shots of John Daniel's potty training.

The lead role is being played by Jasper, who, at the age of seven, is already a veteran of several films, among them *Gorillas in the Mist.* His work schedule is exacting — as a few action-snippets may show.

10.30 am: The chimp wagon pulls into our farmyard. Jasper travels in a cage inside a horse trailer fitted with lights and fan heater. With him come Rona Brown, his trainer who has known him all his life, and his minder, a solid fellow called Mike Vandy. These two form an effective double act. Jasper regards Rona as his mother, and will do anything for her, especially when she bribes or rewards him with fruit, vegetables and sweets. Mike he sees as a father-figure, who may come on heavy if he does not behave.

10.40 am: The camera is set up on the lawn to shoot the privy. 'Right then,' says Rona. 'I'll start winding Jasper up.'

Inside the van the chimp scrambles out of his box and sits on top of it. On goes a child's nappy, then his two-piece gorilla suit. No ordinary garment, it needed four fittings and cost £5,000, being made of Lycra threaded with thousands of knotted yak hairs.

'Hand!' says Rona, and Jasper holds one out. 'Good boy! Foot! Good boy! Push! Other foot! Sit! Good boy!' She talks continuously, as she might to a child. 'Yes,' she tells him about me. 'He's a new face, but you'll like him.' Over her shoulder, Jasper extends a hand. When I take it, he draws my hand over and runs his lower lip minutely across my wrist.

The third human member of his team is Stuart Artingstall, a wig-maker who devised the suit and has cornered the market in disguising animals. As one of the film crew put it: 'If you want to turn an elephant into a mammoth, Stuart's your man.' Now, once the chimp's little gorilla helmet is in position, he darkens the animal's face with vegetable dye, and brushes out his yak-hair.

11.00 am: Jasper rides up to the lawn on Rona's back. The first take is of him walking to the privy hand-in-hand with his mistress, played by the actress Mary Macleod. When all is set, Rona passes his hand to Mary and leaps back out of the camera. 'Action!' calls the producer. The camera rolls. Mary and Jasper advance to the privy and open the door. All is well.

11.20 am: The close-up, of them both enthroned, proves less easy. With his trainer/mother beside him, Jasper will sit still, but the moment Rona yields up her seat to Mary, he is all over the place.

11.35 am: A few days ago, intelligence reached me that Jasper would not sit on anything with a hole in it. I therefore painstakingly cut out a circular piece of board with which to plug the opening in the privy seat. But now he has found that the plug is loose. In a flash he has it up and is groping down the hole. 'Hell!' somebody groans. 'He's half-way down the loo.' More carpentry, then: in a flash we have the loose piece nailed down beneath a sheet of plywood.

12.00 pm: With infinite patience, everyone is still trying for the shot. 'Chimp noises, Stuart!' calls Rona suddenly. 'Hoo-hoo-hoo' goes Stuart from outside the little building. But Jasper is not to be bluffed. In an attempt to distract him, Mary pulls a square of paper from the sheaf on the wall and hands it to him. With both hands, he claps it down on top of his head, then scrumples it in one hand and eats it.

12.25 pm: At last, by dint of giving him a hefty dose of Ribena, Rona gets him to sit still, with his feet dangling and an appropriately inward expression on his face as the drink goes down. The shot is in the can, and we can all break for lunch.

1.45 pm: Jasper is dressing for action again, this time on our kitchen table. In saunters his namesake, Jasper the tabby cat. The chimp gives an abrupt cry. The cat, suddenly aware of a hairy black stranger above him, does two circuits of the table, claws screeching on the flag-stones, clears the bottom half of the stable-type door and vanishes into the orchard at about 30 knots.

2.45 pm: Eleven children from Uley village school, chosen for resembling their predecessors who played with the real John Daniel seventy years ago, are lined up at the bottom of the hill for a scene in which they come walking with the ape along the stream. Since chimps do not like small human beings, and see them as rivals, Rona reads the riot act in words of one syllable: 'When the chimp comes out, you do *not* scream and shout. You do *not* run after him. You do *not* try to touch him . . .'

The children are fascinated, but behave admirably. 'He's a grimp!' one of them cries. 'Half a gorilla and half a chimp.' The grimp, however, loses his nerve and will not walk with Mary when pursued by a crocodile of skipping nippers. Twice he breaks free with loud shrieks and rushes away uphill to fling himself into the arms of his minder. Eventually Rona has to change into period costume and join the crocodile in the guise of the schoolmistress.

So, by fits and starts, the story of John Daniel is recreated. How it will end is not yet certain, for the producer has several options.

Energetic research by the BBC has revealed that there were in fact three John Daniels. The first was the one who lived in Uley, but he came to a sticky end.

Bought for 1,000 guineas — the price of three elephants — by Ringling & Barnum & Bailey's circus, he was taken to New York and briefly exhibited there, but sickened, died, and finished his days, stuffed, in the Natural History Museum, where he still is.

John Daniel II was also exhibited live in New York, where he appeared with his owner in a glass-fronted apartment in Madison Square Garden. His fate is uncertain. JD III was apparently poisoned by a neighbour of Miss Cunningham's in Knightsbridge, who considered that a gorilla lowered the tone in that part of the metropolis.

Stuffed or poisoned? Neither fate would make a cheerful climax. But perhaps it is right that the saga should end in tears, for part of the film's purpose is to show how our attitudes to animals have become more enlightened since the days when Miss Cunningham went shopping at Ponting's.

July

On a Cornish Farm

More than 200 holiday-makers throng the circular viewing gallery, gazing down in rapt fascination as eighteen Friesian cows move slowly round beneath them on the rotating platform of the milking parlour. Light classical music helps the cows relax, and mirrors give the humans a close-up view of events at udder-level. All around are notices explaining the processes and characters on display. Cow No. 58, for instance, is Norma, 'the worst kicker' in the herd. The most popular with visitors is Snowball, No. 104, nicknamed 'How Now' . . .

It was in the early 1970s, fully fifteen years ago, that Rex Davey of Tresillian Barton, near Newquay in Cornwall, became aware of the threats already starting to loom over European agriculture. One of the first to see the dangers of over-production, he was also one of the first to take positive action and do what thousands of other farmers are now belatedly rushing to do — diversify.

Farmer, agricultural engineer, JCB contractor and local character, Rex already had a passion for collecting old engines and equipment, and this proved a major asset when he and his brother Frank decided to open their 550-acre farm to the public. By chance they had recently installed the rotary milking parlour because they considered it the most efficient available. Then they realised it was also the most suitable for spectators; and with that and the embryo museum, they had the beginnings of a new business.

The West Country Tourist Board, eager to create fresh attractions, offered to put up £50,000 for development, provided the Daveys matched the grant with the same amount; but Rex declined the offer, thinking the risk too great, and decided to build the place up slowly instead.

The result is altogether outstanding. The Daveys set out to create an alternative source of income — against the day when milk quotas would cut their normal output — and this they have done. But another of their aims was to promote better understanding between town and country, and in this they have been even more successful.

Today the farm, known as Dairyland, attracts more than 70,000 visitors a year. It has won three major tourist awards, and families not only return year after year, but often make three or four visits in the same season.

The milking parlour remains the central attraction, and could hardly be better organised from either bovine or human point of view. Everything is so well automated that one man can milk 120 cows in an hour: apart from his normal equipment, he has closed-circuit television to show him what is happening out in the collecting yard, and an electric sheep-dog, known as 'K 9', with which he can gently goad laggards forward. The viewing galleries can accommodate 400 people, and such is the wealth of information displayed that any child eager to learn must go away stuffed with facts about a cow's life and metabolism.

Friesians apart, there are numerous other animals — pigs, goats, sheep, horses and rabbits — and a wide variety of birds, including pheasants, hawks and owls. The calves and lambs are so tame that they can be patted or cuddled, and so give some children the first chance they have ever had of touching a live animal.

For sheer furriness and strokeability, nobody at the moment can surpass Denzil (son of Dumpling), the seven-week-old pedigree Shetland pony, who is knee-high to any normal horse, and an utter knock-out. Setting off through his paddock, one can walk a mile-long nature trail to a lake in the valley; and back in the main complex children of all ages happily spend hours digging in various sand-pits with miniature JCBs, built in the farm workshops.

For me, the museum alone would be worth a whole afternoon. Rarely can the aura of the rural past have been so well or powerfully recreated. Part of the magic lies in the fact that almost all the exhibits are local, rescued from close at hand, so that they present an authentic and homogenous picture of Cornish life in days gone by. To Rex Davey, 'collecting things is a hobby that's got completely out of control,' but for visitors his mania is a god-send.

Here is an alcove devoted to poaching, with black metal traps labelled 'Rabbit', 'Otter', 'Badger', 'Deer' and 'Man', and a typical Victorian notice: 'TRESPASSERS BEWARE. During the fruit season, man-traps and spring-guns are placed in this orchard.'

Here are farm implements, water pumps and water-powered engines (all working). Here is an apple mill driven by horse-round, dating from 1800, here a cider press with a circular table (or base) six feet wide, cut from a single piece of granite and made in 1750. Here is a complete blacksmith's shop, an ox-wain of 1800, a Victress Vowel washing machine of 1857, like a butter churn . . .

To me the most evocative object of all is the horse-drawn hearse, long, black and elegant, with glass sides, and beside it the haunting fragment of a poem:

The landsman's coach is jetty black,
   The team has shoulders sore.
The trailing hounds are hanging back,
   Too gaunt to go before.

I had not expected to find a visit to Dairyland so moving. In the end it is neither the great variety of exhibits, both alive and inanimate, nor the neatness of lawns and flowerbeds, nor yet the excellence of the organisation, that make the greatest impact. What really strikes home is the feeling that all this display has been laid on with rare warmth and wit and humanity.

The overwhelming impression created by the farm is that the people who run it are perfectly in tune with their animals and with the environment. To go round the place is to share their harmony with nature, to feel the pulse of country life. Surely it is an extraordinary achievement, and a service of incalculable value, that such a farm should give urban visitors a chance of regaining contact with the past, with their roots, and above all with the land — on which, in the final analysis, every one of us depends.

Giants of the Forest

For anyone who fears that his or her ideas about nature and conservation may be stuck in a rut, there could be no better cure than a trip to California. Everything there is on such a scale as to make our own flora, fauna and ecological problems seem insignificant.

I went to the Yosemite National Park expecting to be impressed. I came away awe-struck, partly by the grandeur of the smooth-capped, vertiginous, granite mountains and the cascading waterfalls, but mostly by the sheer size of the trees.

The giant sequoias have a national park of their own, farther south; but at the bottom end of Yosemite there is a magnificent stand of them known as the Mariposa Grove. I defy anyone with the slightest sense of wonder to visit this magical place and come away unmoved.

Sequoiadendron giganteum lives up to its name. Prime specimens are the largest living objects on earth. Figures scarcely begin to convey their magnificence — but the biggest at Mariposa, known as the Grizzly Giant, is thirty-one feet in diameter at the base. Imagine a single trunk with a diameter almost equal to the width of a tennis court: over ten yards of solid wood and bark.

Vast though it is, the Grizzly Giant is by no means the tallest tree in the grove, for the top seventy-five feet of its trunk were blown off by a lightning strike many years ago, and it now reaches little more than 200 feet. Many of its neighbours, better proportioned and more elegant, rise straight as red-brown gun-barrels to a height of almost 300.

Yet it was neither their size nor their grace which impressed me most. The really stunning fact about them is their age. To us, in England, a 300-year old oak is a rarity, a moribund 1,000-year old yew a miraculous object. Yet among the giant sequoias such antiquity is as nothing.

Truncated though it may be, the Grizzly Giant is 2,700 years old and going strong. I found it extraordinary to stand in the presence of a colossus which was already old when Sir Francis Drake landed on the coast of California in 1579, middle-aged in the time of Charlemagne, still in its youth when Christ was crucified, and perhaps even growing as a sapling when Homer wrote the *Iliad*. What is man in the face of such tremendous longevity?

Everything about the sequoias and their management seems to be on an heroic scale. Their roots fan out so far laterally — to stabilise the tremendous weight above — that one tree's support-system may cover two acres and draw over 1,000 gallons of water from the soil every day.

When European explorers discovered the giants in the 1850s, early conservationists misguidedly sought to protect them by suppressing the forest fires started by lightning strikes in late summer and autumn. Nobody then realised that sequoias are naturally protected against fire by the thickness of their spongy bark (up to two feet), and that fire plays a vital role in the regeneration of the species.

Now it is known that three things are essential for the seedlings of these giants to germinate: direct sunlight on the forest floor, adequate moisture, and bare mineral soil. When natural fires were repeatedly extinguished, shade-tolerant trees such as white firs, incense cedars and sugar pines quickly spread, competing for moisture and blanketing the ground with their fallen needles, so that it became impossible for sequoia seedlings to get a start.

Not until the 1960s did the park rangers realise what was happening. By then more than 100 years' worth of unburnt litter and young evergreens had built up: had lightning ignited such a depth of tinder, the resulting blaze might have been so fierce as to kill even the mature trees.

To forestall any such disaster, a programme of controlled burns was started in spring and autumn — and the results were excellent. Intrusive pine seedlings and leaf-litter were burnt off, leaving the ground bare. The heat of the fires dried out cones high in the mature trees, causing them to open and scatter seeds on to the newly prepared bed below. Then winter snow-storms buried the land under a deep white blanket, and when this melted in the spring, moisture percolated down to make the seeds germinate. The result, today, is that many glades in the grove are carpeted by bright-green saplings.

Fire is used as a management tool in other areas of Yosemite as well. In the words of an official leaflet, it is the goal of park managers 'to let fire continue to shape the landscape'. Yet by no means every blaze is deliberate. Information boards tersely chart the progress of a major outbreak in the summer of 1990 which left more than 25,000 acres of forest destroyed.

On 7 August, twenty-eight separate lightning strikes raked one flank of the Yosemite valley. By the following day 1,900 acres of forest were alight. On the 9th, a 60 mph wind produced a firestorm, and 480 fire-fighters were drafted in to contain it. On the 10th, 15,000 visitors had to be evacuated from the valley in four hours; by the 11th, 3,000 fire-fighters were in action, and eleven million dollars had been spent.

In California, as I say, nature seems to operate on a grand scale. Yet anyone in search of arboreal height-records must go further up the Pacific Coast, to the redwood forests north of San Francisco.

Even if they lack the sheer bulk of their relations the sequoias, redwoods are still taller, reaching a height — inconceivable in Britain — of nearly 400 feet. To walk in cool, resin-scented shade among the soaring columns of their trunks is to wander though a cathedral as glorious as any made by man: to consider their antiquity is — again — a humbling experience.

At the entrance to one of the trails in the Armstrong Grove, near the Russian River, there stands on edge a slice sawn from the trunk of a redwood felled by vandals in 1978. Pointers fixed to the annual growth-rings in its face give an idea of the history which the life of this tree encompassed: 1861, the American Civil War; 1620, the Pilgrim fathers arrive at Plymouth Rock; 1066, William the Conqueror invades England; 948, germination of this tree.

I was delighted to find — in passing — that the humus which builds up on the forest floor is known in these parts as 'duff', and that the stuff has a vital part to play in the life of the redwoods. 'Duff also acts as a mulch . . . Duff/humus is a vital link in the ecology.'

For sheer antiquity, however, everything pales before another wonder close by — the petrified forest. Three million years ago the volcano now known as Mount St Helena blew up, and the eruption first flattened, then buried in ash, the redwoods for miles around.

Today some of those trees have been dug out for man to wonder at — and amazing they are. To the eye, they are still wood, with every detail of bark, knots, cracks, breaks and wormholes perfectly preserved. To the finger or the cheek, they are stone. To lay your face against a tree three million years old makes present worries seem very small.

What would Blind Homer have written, could he have touched these stone survivors? In one of the most famous passages of the *Iliad,* he compared the generations of men with those of leaves, one springing up as another dies. The idea of stone trees, surviving from the unimaginably distant past, would surely have inspired him to lines equally immortal.

Sandy's Special Rides

When Sandy Steel says 'off road', he means it. Away we went, pedalling straight out of the Cotswold village of Eastleach and into a hairy, uneven meadow. Of the bridle-path marked on the map, there was not a trace.

No matter. The wilder the going, the better Sandy liked it. Through a gate and down the edge of a barley-field we bounced; a second gate, and we were dropping along the edge of another meadow into an enchanting little valley. At the bottom a curious double-gate and causeway led us across what looked like a derelict watercress bed, carved from the course of the infant river Leach.

Then we turned left, up steep grass banks, heading for the corner of a spinney. At last a track of sorts appeared, between a field of barley and the trees, but it was choked with thistles, stinging nettles and docks seven feet high. 'Ah!' said Sandy, his eyes lighting up. 'This looks more like it.'

A tall, engagingly eccentric man of thirty-two, with receding hair and long, powerful legs, he was reconnoitring the latest of the numerous cross-country trails which his passion for off-road bicycling has led him to pioneer. His firm Steelaway specialises in sending out parties up to thirty strong to explore the landscape by means of bridleways, farm-tracks, towpaths, disused railways and (as little as possible) single-track lanes.

Most of the rides are centred round his own base, a cottage near Cirencester, but many go farther afield: the Upper Thames, Wiltshire white horses, Cotswolds to Salisbury, and, most ambitious of all, Buckingham Palace to Bath — a three-day marathon of 120 miles, only five of which are on proper roads.

Sandy's own obsession with cycling derived indirectly from the fact that he was cursed with dyslexia — a condition not remedied until it had wrecked his schooling. (He still reads slowly, and has difficulty visualising more than two letters at a time.)

Leaving Rugby prematurely, he was expected to become an accountant, but could not manage the bookwork, and so took a series of increasingly menial jobs in London — about thirty in all. The last was at Crufts' dog show, where he ended up 'as a security guard guarding the guard-dogs, the Dobermann Pinschers'.

By then his parents had retired to Gloucestershire, and he took to cycling out at weekends, eighty miles each way. Because he could not bear going along the same roads all the time, he tried different ones: first the A roads, then the hard shoulders of motorways.

These seemed to him excellent: the surfaces were first-class, the gradients admirably engineered. As he puts it, 'the wind of the Friday traffic used to sweep me towards Gloucestershire.'

Not everyone, however, shared his enthusiasm. He attributes his demise to the advent of the car telephone, which some busybody must have used to alert the constabulary. One day, waiting to intercept him on the crest just before the Marlow/High Wycombe exit from the M 40, was a policeman, who ordered him off.

Gradually he became fascinated by the idea of finding a way out of London not along arterial roads. First he tried, and failed, using an A-Z. He thought he could 'twiddle down, shoot out between two last mock-Tudor houses, and see cows browsing in a field' — but these tactics only landed him in Southall at dead of night.

Then, with the advent of the mountain bike five years ago, he became more ambitious, and bought a set of Ordnance Survey 1:50,000 maps covering the whole of London. Using them, and clinging to the Thames towpath as much as possible, he found his way from Hammersmith to Windsor without going on a road at all, except to cross bridges.

The bug was into him. He worked out off-road routes right through London, east-west, north-south, and reckoned that if he could so dissect the metropolis, he could go anywhere.

Then he bought a small cottage in the country, and set up his present operation three years ago. He now has thirty bikes of his own, which he hires out, and a van and trailer specially fitted so that he can transport twenty-four of them at once.

His rates are modest. He charges £15 a day for the hire of a cycle, including a marked-up map and instruction about the route. Each machine comes fully equipped with pannier, tool kit, spare inner tube, water-bottle and a handlebar pouch which acts as a miniature lectern for holding the map in front of you. If you bring your own bike, he charges the ridiculous fee of £6 for his expertise. He will also sell you a bike, new or secondhand, and finds that more and more clients buy the one they have ridden.

The key to the whole operation is the map, laminated on both sides so as to be fully weatherproof, and with the day's route marked in detail. Before a group sets out, Sandy talks the leaders through the day to make sure they understand the less familiar symbols — for instance, a colourless road can be a lane, a drive leading to a house or farm, or just a farm track.

His clients vary enormously. The professionals, who turn up in lycra shorts to race, cover sixty miles a day; but, as he points out, 'you can have a jolly nice day and do fifteen'. A third of his customers are foreign tourists. Americans in particular are bowled over by the chance of taking to woods and fields — for in the United States there is no tradition or system of footpaths, bridleways, such as we have in Britain, and the only places in which one can ride off-road are national parks, which are swarming with other tourists.

That, for most riders, is the point of off-road biking: to escape into the country and get clean away from traffic and other people. Until I went out with Sandy, I had not appreciated the extent to which this is possible — even though I have an all-terrain bike of my own and live in the Cotswolds.

Our reconnaissance led us in a left-handed sweep round Macaroni Downs, where Regency bucks would come out from Cheltenham to gamble on cockfights. In a ride of over two hours, we were on a lane for only one short stretch, and we scarcely saw a human being or a machine. Through spinneys, along the headlands of cornfields, past deserted farmyards, with hares gambolling ahead of us and partridges springing from the wheat, we cruised through marvellously deep country. No matter that squalls of heavy drizzle swept over us: they merely softened the mud and made the going more interesting.

Throughout the ride Sandy kept up a diverting commentary — on local history as much as on the curious legal status of the bicyclist. One moment he was describing how Shelley, wanting to row along the Thames-Severn canal in 1815, was so outraged by the lock-keeper's demand for a fee of £20 that he abandoned his proposed journey and wrote a poem instead. The next, he was discoursing on the fact that, because bicycles post-date all laws and rights for horse-riders and pedestrians, they occupy a grey legal area, and no one is sure what rights their users have.

What seems certain is that he has pioneered an admirably inoffensive method of allowing people to enjoy the countryside. In two full years of operation, Steelaway has attracted no complaint, and provoked no confrontation — and I did notice, looking back, that for ninety per cent of our trial route we left no trace of our passing.

Hut for a Hermit

Walking out early the other morning, I made a detour to the spot on which, if I owned the land, I should build my writing-hut. It is a small clearing on a spur in the middle of a wood, and commands a fine view of farmland in the valley below; its magic is that it has exactly the right combination of secrecy and openness, of intimacy with the forest and visual access to the farmland, which my ideal site demands.

The dream of having a writing-hut has haunted me for years. My idea is that I should establish a second work-station out in the wilds, far from telephones and visitors, to which I should walk out after breakfast, and in which I should settle down for the rest of the morning, spurred on to compose deathless prose by the idyllic nature of my surroundings.

In fact I am not so naive as to suppose things would work out like that. As with any form of outdoor existence — camping, for instance — the mere business of supporting life takes up so much time and energy that little remains for more intellectual activities. Brewing mid-morning coffee, for instance, is a far longer job in the wilds than in the kitchen.

Although my woodland den would consist basically of a garden hut, it would need to have certain embellishments, among them extremely stout foundations, so that it could withstand the winter storms, and an inner skin of tongued-and-grooved pine planking, to give it adequate insulation and a comfortable feel.

I should also want a miniature wood-burning stove, to make the place snug in cold weather, and a big window at which I could sit, looking out. These would mean, in turn, some form of chimney, and a heavy, vandal-proof shutter, to protect the window in my absence. Inside, I should want a flat surface beneath the window, on which to work, and a bed or hammock on which to recline when inspiration failed.

None of this would be difficult to achieve: I see myself buying a regular garden hut, refurbishing it at home, staining the outside a suitable grey-green, dismantling the whole thing into sections, and transporting them out to the site with tractor and trailer. But the site, the site! That is the key element in the exercise.

For years I fancied one at the head of our nearest stream, in a coign of the high grassland, where, all the year round, a spring bubbles out of the hillside over a bed of gravel, and a rivulet of crystal water sets off on its journey towards the Severn. The place has almost everything in its favour: isolation, protection from the prevailing west wind, grand views, and, of course, the wherewithal for making tea or coffee. Its only drawback is that it is in open country, with no trees nearby — and some atavistic instinct makes me want to be surrounded by forest.

The other site, which I visited this week, is certainly that. Only the very nose of the spur is clear. All round — behind, at the sides and in front below — are protective walls of ash, oak, hazel, beech and other species. Because the land up there is poor, and full of stone, the trees tend to be stunted; but this means only that they have short trunks, and that their foliage is closer to the ground than it would be on more favourable soil, making them a more effective screen.

The owner of the wood, who lives some distance away, has kindly given me permission to walk through his property. Having met him only once, I scarcely know him; but one fact which makes me warm to him is that he clearly shares my predilection for escaping into the forest.

He already *has* a hut in the wood, fitted up almost exactly as I have described, with the addition of an old cask set on end to catch rainwater piped off the roof. When he was younger, he used often to spend the night there — and perhaps he still does from time to time.

His hut is not on the elevated spot which I like best, but deep in a re-entrant, buried in a sea of tall beeches, with no view at all and very little sun. It also has the further disadvantage — in my eyes — of standing close by a footpath.

Why then did the owner choose to build it there? I could perfectly well ask him, but somehow I never have. What I can infer, however, is that he has designs of a sort on the higher site, for he has made a jeepable track, curving through the hazel, which approaches to within fifty yards of it, and on the spur itself he has cut one or two small trees to extend the clearing and improve its outlook.

At 7.30 on a fine autumn morning, the place was everything I could hope for. Except for the cooing of pigeons, silence reigned. Heavy dew lay undisturbed on the grass, and the only indication of a recent visitor was the stripped bark of an ash-sapling, frayed by a roebuck establishing his territory.

I sat down for a few minutes to enjoy the view and to think how agreeable it would be to work in such a place. Away in the distance to my right shrill whistles started to echo about the head of the valley as the resident family of young buzzards launched into their morning flight-trials. I began to think of the old stone farmhouse which once occupied the end of the valley beneath my feet: fifteen years ago, for reasons best known to himself, the farmer flattened it and bulldozed the remains underground, thereby depriving himself of at least £100,000 . . .

Something invaded my reverie. I could smell woodsmoke. With the wind in the west, it could not be coming from the village over the hill behind. No foresters were at work that early. In those steep hills the air-currents are often baffling — but the only possible source seemed to be the woodland owner's hut in the end of the valley below.

Was he in residence, then? I became intensely curious. It would take only a couple of minutes to walk round the top of the wood, down the footpath and straight past his front door . . . yet somehow I felt that it would be wrong to disturb him. If he was there, he had clearly come for the isolation, and to break it would be boorish.

Keeping the dogs well in, I therefore went round on a higher path, to a point from which I could see straight down through the trees to the roof of his hut. Again I sat down to watch. Now the breeze was coming straight up the face from below, yet no smell of smoke was reaching me. Besides, through binoculars I could see the little stovepipe chimney in detail, and nothing was emerging from it.

One thing will settle this, I thought: if I wind bacon frying, I will know he's there. But that magical morning smell never materialised, and in the end I decided that the hut was empty.

Where had the woodsmoke come from, then? I never found out, but beat a discreet retreat. My theory of moving through a forest is that one should make oneself as inconspicuous and evanescent as the wild creatures which live there: walk through, by all means, but go slowly, keep as quiet as the deer, and when you leave, slip silently away, so that you leave the spirit of the place intact.

My hut — if ever I build it — will inevitably seem alien at first. But experience shows that wild creatures take very little notice of man-made structures, provided no noisy activities take place in them, and soon accept them as part of the forest. That would be my aim: to sit and work in the heart of the wood, with its denizens paying me no attention.

Nature Strikes Back

To walk over the Army gunnery ranges at Lulworth, in Dorset — which one can do only if specially accompanied — is like going back 100 years, or even 500. This rough ground is surely what much of England looked like in the Middle Ages: it must have been this kind of terrain over which Bosworth Field, Sedgemoor and a hundred other battles were fought.

In a word, the texture of the landscape is *hairy.* The grassland is unkempt, sprouting weeds and wild flowers. Thickets of blackthorn and gorse spread impenetrably, and the hedges have so long run riot that they consist not of bushes but of full-grown trees, many of which, though still alive, are reclining horizontally from a combination of age and exhaustion. The woods themselves have reverted to tangled primeval forest, much of it impassable.

In ecological terms, the ranges form one of the most fascinating areas in England, for the land has never been touched by herbicides, insecticides or artificial fertilisers, and much of it has not been farmed — except by intermittent grazing — for seventy years. The result is that it supports flora and fauna not to be found elsewhere.

The ranges cover 7,500 acres, straddling the western end of the Isle of Purbeck, and include some spectacular scenery. Along their six miles of coast are tremendous cliffs, the remains of a fossilised forest, and lovely bays.

Immediately inland, majestic chalk ridges clad in short grass run parallel to the shore; inland from them stretches a huge heath, some of it wet peat bog, some dry.

The Army began firing here during the First World War, when it took a lease of the Bindon area, some 2,500 acres next to Lulworth Cove. In 1938, the lease was extended for ninety-nine years; but then, in 1943, as the improvement in tank weapons demanded longer practice ranges, the Army requisitioned another 5,000 acres to the east and evacuated 100 families, many from the village of Tyneham, which lies in a lovely valley running down to the sea.

Forty-five years later, the speed with which the evacuation was carried out, and the easy promises which accompanied it, have been neither forgotten nor forgiven. The order was issued at the end of December 1942, and everybody had to leave their homes within twenty-eight days. The families went on the clear understanding that they would be allowed back as soon as the emergency was over — but after the war, the Army ratted on the agreement, sat tight, and acquired the whole area by compulsory purchase.

Hopes of a return rose in 1970, when a major study of lands held by the Ministry of Defence recommended that Lulworth should be handed back to civilian use; but this decision was later rescinded, partly because the military claimed that the ranges were irreplaceable, and partly because the task of making the ground safe had by then become almost impossibly difficult.

Very little bursting ammunition is fired nowadays, but so many high-explosive shells have been used over the years that many blind rounds, which failed to go off, must be buried in the ground, and it would take hundreds of man-years of effort to clear the land. The military thus feel that it can never be opened to the public, and that they will be there for the foreseeable future.

Wild creatures evidently feel the same. In spite of prodigious noise, from the crackle of small arms to the thunder of 120mm anti-tank weapons, the ranges are teeming with foxes, badgers, deer of three kinds (sika, roe and fallow) and lesser denizens such as the natterjack toad. The gunnery school runs two successful pheasant shoots, and the army branch of the British Deer Society has to work hard to keep the herd down to an acceptable level.

Birds of all kinds flourish, from the gannets on the coast to the buzzards, hobbies, larks, stone-chats and Dartford warblers of the interior. In the absence of chemical warfare waged by farmers, insect life is of an abundance found in few other places. Butterflies frequent the chalk-land by the hundred — marbled white, dark green fritillary, meadow brown gatekeeper, Lulworth skipper — along with many species of cricket, and dragonflies which skim the peat bog inland. Altogether, 124 species of moth have been identified, 353 of beetle and sixty-seven of spider.

Even to a layman, the vegetation is extraordinary. Huge wild cabbages, with leaves as thick and tough as parchment, sprout in the ragged fields. In the spring, wild garlic bursts out all over. Clumps of daffodils and bamboo mark spots where cottage gardens flourished long ago.

Because of all this, the ranges are of compelling interest to the Nature Conservancy Council, which has declared most of them sites of special scientific interest and the whole area is in effect a more or less unmanaged nature reserve, whose peculiar status puts the Army into a difficult position.

Forbidden by the NCC to make changes without consulting the scientists, the military are faced with an insoluble dilemma. What, in conservation terms, are they supposed to be doing? Should they simply let everything go to jungle, or should they try to preserve some semblance of order?

The problem is poignantly evident in the ruins of Tyneham village. The church is almost intact, for it still belongs to the Church Commissioners, and its roof has been maintained. But forty-five years of weather, neglect and vandalism have reduced the houses to stumpy walls, not much more than one storey high. There is something terribly sad about these little shells of homes, whose inhabitants were so suddenly whisked away.

The Army has capped the walls with cement, to prevent further decay, and now aims to preserve the village indefinitely. Yet to what end? No one can say exactly — but the military are certainly anxious to atone in any way possible for the inhuman treatment which the people of Tyneham received in the past.

To an outsider, the most striking fact about Lulworth is the power with which nature hits back when man, for whatever reason, is prevented from exercising his usual destructive bent; and it seems particularly ironic that here the element allowing nature's comeback is the torrent of high-velocity shells that go whistling overhead.

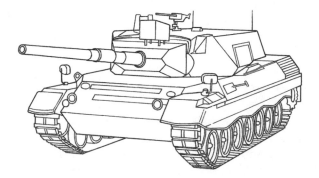

August

Wild Life Artists

From now until 11 August the annual exhibition of the Society of Wildlife Artists will be open at the Mall Galleries in London. With more than 550 works on display, this is the biggest show the society has ever staged in its twenty-eight-year history, and, as always, some frantic last-minute activity attended its preparation: to lay their hands on one set of bird pictures by the distinguished Swedish artist Lars Jonsson, for instance, the organisers had to make a dash to Heathrow and fork out over £1,000 in VAT to HM Customs.

Yet the most vital preliminary took place in May, when the selection committee met to sift through the immense drift of paintings sent in for consideration from every corner of the kingdom. The Society's seventy-odd members are allowed to submit ten each, but, besides these home-grown offerings, more than 500 works had poured in from hopeful outsiders — and if the artists had heard half the remarks which their masterpieces elicited from the panel, many of them might never have set brush to canvas or paper again.

The committee met in a basement room of a very grand house in Carlton House Terrace. No doubt cooks or scullery maids used to toil down there in days gone by; but on that morning in May eight good men and true, four of them bearded, sat elbow-to-elbow on chairs along one wall, facing a long, padded bench on which the pictures were to be displayed, and a team of art-students hovered in the background, ready to present each work in turn.

Proceedings were opened by the Society's President, Robert Gillmor, himself a bird-painter of wide repute — a comfortable figure in thick sweater and trainers, whose bald head and stocky build at once conjured up images of Friar Tuck. Sitting on the bench in front of the panel, feet dangling, he sketched the rules with a minimum of formality:

'There are eight of us voting. Six votes will mean A, or accepted. Five will be D, or doubtful. Anything with four or less is out. We've already got 353 works by members. That means we can't take more than 200 by non-members — but 554 have been submitted. In other words, we need well under half.'

The students swung into action, holding each picture upright on the bench for the judges to scrutinise. If one artist had submitted several works, all came up together.

Stunned silence greeted the first batch of three. At last someone said incredulously, 'Is that meant to be an owl?' Another silence, after which Gillmor asked, 'No votes at all?' and motioned the whole lot away.

The second batch was of two pictures. 'That elephant looks very ill indeed,' remarked someone acidly. 'It's sub-Babar.'

'They want £5,500 for it,' said a voice from the background.

'Do they, by God!'

Again, not a vote, and away went the ailing pachyderm. The girl who presented it maintained an admirably non-committal expression — but was there not a hint of contempt, of barely-suppressed derision, on the face of the boy who brought the next offering?

Not until the eighth painting did interest perk up. 'Ah!' said Gillmor suddenly. 'I think we've got something here. The grebe's all right, isn't it? What about the fox, though?'

One painting showed a grebe on a nest with its mate swimming nearby. The other was of an immensely solid fox in the snow. 'They do get pretty thick coats in the winter,' said a doubtful voice, countered at once by, '*I* thought it was a wolf.'

'Can we vote for the fox?' asked Gillmor. 'One? Two? No — the fox is out. Right: we'll have the grebes.'

As the panel warmed up, their comments became less and less inhibited. 'That was a nice piece of paper, once . . . I wouldn't like to meet that woodcock on a dark night . . . Here the background's fighting the foreground . . . Ah! A badger up a tree. Oh no — it's a panda.'

Behind the frivolity and occasional waspishness lay a serious purpose: to choose pictures which showed that the artists had some real knowledge of their subjects. Photographic realism was *not* what the panel wanted. As Gillmor explained in an aside, 'There has to be some quality of design and composition, of course. But what we're really after is a feeling for the way an animal or bird lives and breathes and moves. It doesn't matter if a picture is highly impressionistic, so long as it says something about the subject's behaviour.'

On an outsider, the cumulative effect soon became claustrophobic. Some of the paintings were nightmarish, some merely enormous, some both. One vast, Rousseau-ish fantasy was so huge that it could not stand upright in the eight feet or so of headroom above the bench.

On they came in droves: butterflies, squirrels, hedgehogs, stoats, otters, coots, goosanders, duck, geese, woodpeckers, flamingos, a cassowary head-on, lions, elephants, whales, deer, Tasmanian devils, colossal snakes bursting from their frames. On the whole, the studies of birds were most successful, perhaps because birds are most easily observed.

Much work had obviously been done in zoos, a good deal in Africa. Somehow the idea of wild creatures being so intensively fancied became slightly alarming. The only class of animals which had escaped scrutiny was that of domestic pets, which were specifically excluded. No cats, dogs or horses, therefore, but almost everything else.

Tigers especially: tigers of every size and shape, burning bright, asleep, roaring. Loud groans greeted the appearance of yet another striped feline, apparently being sick into a ditch. 'Last year was the year of the hedgehog,' somebody observed. 'We had hedgehogs coming out of our ears. This is the year of the tiger.'

The procession seemed never-ending. 'Will you vote for the coypu?' called Gillmore above the hubbub. 'No — you won't'. Some pictures were dismissed because the artists had deliberately aped the style of masters like the late Sir Peter Scott, others because they were clearly done from photographs. Altogether the carnage was fearful. 'That's an interesting . . . bit of framing . . . What the hell's THAT? (of a mass of grey and white feathers on an orange background). 'A woodpigeon? It looks like it's been hit by a tram.'

So it went on, until 184 pictures had been chosen and more than 350 consigned to oblivion. The atmosphere, though critical, remained good-natured and constructive — for the jurors knew full well that, when the show opened, they might easily be cornered by the infuriated daubers whose work they had thrown out.

'I have a dread of being trapped in a corner at the Private View,' confessed Keith Shackleton, the veteran bird artist. 'People come up quite belligerently and demand to know why their pictures haven't been hung.

'I always say, "Well, you know, it's a democratic process, and I'm afraid the vote just went against you.' And then they say, in a very menacing voice, "You should *just understand* that I sell this stuff like hot cakes in my own neighbourhood. I'm very well respected . . . "

'So then I answer, "Good!, That's the best bet: sell locally." And the next thing is, they round on me and shout, "I didn't come here to take advice from YOU!"'

Well — the Private View took place on Thursday. Has anyone checked to make sure that Mr. Shackleton is still at liberty?

Badger, Basil & Co.

For anyone who owns a gun-dog, it was a day to remember: a practical seminar on canine psychology, held in the green and peaceful acres of Pinkney Park, near Malmesbury, to raise funds for that admirable organisation, the Game Conservancy. Thirty-two labradors, retrievers and spaniels came along for instruction and/or analysis from two leading trainers, but it was undoubtedly the humans who benefited most.

Sitting on the lawn outside the house, we were enthralled by a talk from Jack Davey, a highly knowledgeable and entertaining expert from Devon. Never a professional trainer, but what he himself describes as an enthusiastic amateur, he worked for forty years as a pest-control officer for the Ministry of Agriculture, and is now retired.

He it was who grappled with the celebrated break-out of porcupines in the West Country: a pregnant female escaped, and only after six years and the capture of eight specimens could Jack and his colleagues be sure that they had stifled another invasion of the English countryside by an alien species, potentially as damaging as those of coypu, mink and grey squirrels.

But Jack was not talking about porcupines. His subject was gundogs, and how to dominate them. 'I don't like using that word,' he said, 'but I have to, because that's what it's all about: domination.'

His central message was that dogs are pack animals, and instinctively look to their pack-leader for guidance and control. Therefore, a human owner must become a pack-leader. 'It's all-important to a dog to have a leader: without one, he can't function.'

Ideally, an owner should take charge of a new puppy when it is seven weeks old, and no more. At that age, it will transfer its mother-bond to its new mistress or master, who will then naturally become its pack-leader.

'What you have to do,' Jack said, 'is bring your own level of intelligence down to that of the dog. Don't expect the dog's intelligence to come anywhere near yours, and don't expect it to have any reasoning power.

'For animals, dogs are highly intelligent, but they can't *think* like we can. They operate on instincts and impulses — and those instincts and impulses work extremely fast: there's no pause for thought between impulse and action. Therefore you, as trainer, have got to react extremely fast as well, and be 101 per cent alert . . .'

An outburst of barking from the lime avenue, where owners' cars were stationed in the shade, with dogs on board, may or may not have signified a protest. But Jack went on imperturbably to point out that training consists essentially of harnessing natural instincts — developing those which help humans, and curbing those which do not.

For a dog, it is natural and enjoyable to hunt, chase, catch and kill prey, and then to carry whatever has been captured back to the pack leader. Clearly one wants a gun-dog to hunt, catch and bring back, but at the same time you must modify its impulse to chase, so that it hunts where you want it to, and suppress that to kill.

The basic essential is therefore control. How do you achieve this? By establishing yourself firmly as pack leader, starting early, working regularly, and making things simple for the pupil. One of Jack's golden rules is that although you may exercise dogs in groups, you should always train them singly.

Words of command should be short, clear and as few as possible — *Sit!*, *Here!*, *Come!*, *Fetch!*, *Heel!*. But the best command of all, the sharpest and least mistakable, is a shot. At first you reinforce the order '*Sit!*' by raising your hand above your head, palm to the dog; and when, after a few hundred repetitions of this, he is obeying instantly, you accompany the raising of the hand by a shot from a starting-pistol. Again, a few hundred repetitions, and he should drop on his haunches whenever he hears a bang . . .

My mind drifted off to the lunatic behaviour of my own labrador, Pansy, now eleven and incorrigibly wild. To her, a shot is a signal not to sit down but to take off — and this she does, unless forcibly restrained, in whatever direction she happens to be facing when she hears the detonation. Clearly the fault it mine, rather than hers, but where did I go wrong? Almost certainly, in starting her on real game too young . . .

Now Jack was on to the vital question of punishment. The best method of chastisement, he said, is to grip a dog by the scruff of its neck and shake it, as its mother would. But the essential point is that punishment must follow misdemeanour instantaneously — otherwise the dog does not connect the two. If your spaniel retrieves someone else's pheasant, the moment for punishment has passed: you should have stopped the dog running-in in the first place.

After an hour and a half of theory, admirably put, the company moved down to the edge of the lake for a practical demonstration by Jack, his son Alan, and their four-year-old spaniel Bess. This could only be described as magisterial. The bitch obeyed every command at once, followed hand-signals precisely, hunted for canvas dummies with immense enthusiasm, and ignored red-herrings dragged across her bows.

Who could argue with Jack after such a show? June Atkinson, the golden retriever specialist, for one. A tall and angular lady, whose gentle voice and manner belie her slightly formidable appearance, she at once said that she trains dogs in pairs, and a good-natured exchange of views broke out.

Her own demonstration — first with two young retrievers, then with two older ones — was scarcely less impressive, and showed that more than one approach is possible. Yet she too was most definitely leader of her pack, and had them under perfect control.

At lunch (also on the lawn) several people laid their problems before Carolyn Nicolle, a local trainer of renown. Besides keeping four spaniels and a labrador of her own, she takes in three or four outsiders at a time and keeps them for six months, charging up to £500 apiece for a complete education. During that time, the owners are not allowed to make contact with their dogs: they may come and watch them performing from discreet vantage-points, but Carolyn allows no closer approach, for fear that it would damage the bond which she has established with her pupils.

Few owners realise how easy it is to wreck or lose the finger-tip control achieved by skilled training. But the specialists agree that if an owner does not continue to exercise proper pack-leadership, and keep up regular routines, a dog theoretically worth £2,000 can go to pot in as little as two months after returning home.

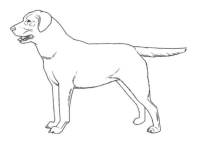

And so to the afternoon: out came several Badgers, one Soda (but no Whisky), one Basil, and a couple of dozen others, predominantly black, but some golden. After the high-class displays in the morning, owners seemed remarkably reluctant to be first in action; but after a while they got going under the benevolent supervision of the two guest experts, and in the event the dogs performed remarkably well. Only once was June Atkinson constrained to let fly a tremendous shout of 'NO!', which stopped one Badger in his tracks.

Proceedings closed with cucumber sandwiches and a polished address from Wilson Stephens, former Editor of *The Field*; who praised the general standard of behaviour; but I think that the dogs had long since got wind of the fact that they were in the presence of a psychoanalyst, and had decided to outwit him by being on their best behaviour.

Saving the Nene

All this week, from eight in the morning until 10.30 at night, an international team of scientists has been slaving away at the Slimbridge Wildfowl and Wetlands Trust, on the water-meadows beside the Severn, crunching numbers in their computers to predict the future of the world's waterfowl.

Outside the big windows of their conference-room, duck were constantly taking off, wheeling across the sky and dropping into the ponds of the sanctuary created by the late Sir Peter Scott. Swans floated on the water, and geese stood about on the grass banks. The scene was idyllic, marred only by the fact that the team indoors was plotting the demise of threatened species.

This sounds a gloomy way of describing their activity — but in fact they were doing exactly that: under the guidance of Professor Ulysses Seal, an expert from the International Union for the Conservation of Nature, they were processing all available information to find out when various endangered species will go extinct unless man steps up his efforts to save them.

A simple chart — the Mace-Lande Criteria for Priority Categories — gave guidance on what to expect with bird-populations of various sizes. Any species numbering 10,000 or more is considered safe. Any with fewer than 250 members, by contrast, is regarded as 'critical', and will go extinct in ten years if left unsupported. Between these extremes are those with 250-2,500 members ('endangered') and 2,500-10,000 ('vulnerable').

The end-product of the week's exercise will be a document sent out to every zoo in the world, advising bird-keepers on how their resources can most profitably be deployed.

Although many species were considered, special attention was focussed on the Nene, pronounced *Naynay* or Hawaiian goose, with which Slimbridge has been involved for more than forty years. A handsome and dignified bird, with black top to its head, barred brown-and-white back, and buff-coloured breast, the Nene is unique in several respects, not least the shape of its feet. These, having less web than those of other waterfowl, make it exceptionally nimble on land, and an excellent walker.

Nenes were once extremely plentiful. The explorer James Cook found them such good meat that he filled the *Resolution* with them during his visit in 1778, and even in this century they featured on the menus of local restaurants. It was Sir Peter Scott himself who brought the birds into the international limelight in 1950, when he discovered that only thirty individuals remained in the wild, and 20-odd in captivity. He promptly sent an expert to help the Hawaiians set up a breeding programme, and the emissary brought back two geese to found a reserve community in England.

These pioneers had been grandly named after members of the former Hawaiian royal family. But when, in the spring, they both began to lay eggs, it became clear that error had crept in. Urgent telegrams produced a gander, raising the British population to three, and from that modest base a whole new tribe has sprung.

There was a low period when the geese passed through what scientists call a 'genetic bottleneck': fertility fell, and eggs failed to hatch. Many species go under when they reach this critical stage, but the Nenes came through it and drew away again so strongly that 200 could be sent back to Hawaii and released on the island of Maui, along with the same number of birds reared locally.

The spearhead of the Nene Recovery Action Group is Dr Jeff Black, a young American waterfowl ecologist who has been at Slimbridge for ten years and is now the establishment's principal research officer. Something of a migrant himself, he follows geese all over the world: he has already made two field trips to Hawaii, and plans another for this winter.

His observations show that in their native habitat Nenes live a most comfortable life. They wake up with the sun and graze for two or three hours on grass, berries or the shoots of other plants. Then, as the sun grows too hot for their liking, they move into the shade and remain there all day, 'basically doing nothing but panting', and not shifting except to keep in their chosen patch of shade. In the evening they graze again before going to sleep. Their one great failing is that they are so tame: even now, after being hunted and shot for centuries, they allow people to come within thirty yards — easy range.

Thanks largely to the efforts of Slimbridge and the Hawaiian biologists, the population in Hawaii has climbed back to 500, but this week's computer simulation showed even that to be not a viable amount: without increased human back-up, the species will die out in twenty years. One important aim of the research group was therefore to suggest ways of stepping up support.

The trouble is that in Hawaii much has changed for the worse since the rescue programme was launched. Not only has a great deal of habitat been destroyed for the benefit of pineapples, sugar cane and hotels: many alien creatures have been imported, some inadvertently, some through misguided attempts to correct the balance of nature.

One deliberate and disastrous introduction was that of the mongoose, brought in to kill rats. The mongoose has now established itself as a major menace, and preys heavily on the young geese. So do feral cats and dogs, and even wild boar, which were imported to provide sport, but bred out of control in the scrub on the mountains.

Another unwelcome immigrant has been the mosquito, which came in on ships and brought with it blood parasites, which killed off all the birds below 1,000 feet. The remaining Nenes sought sanctuary at higher altitudes, and, because the survivors were found high in the mountains, scientists mistakenly thought that this was their natural habitat. Only in recent years has it been appreciated that the geese fare better at a lower level, where the feeding is richer.

Much can be done to help the Nenes survive: predator control programmes can be launched, more geese can be reared in captivity, and better habitat found for those which are released. Many other species of wildfowl are in worse trouble than them — for instance the white-winged wood duck, of which barely 200 are thought to survive.

This week's study gave a fascinating glimpse of the global efforts being made to save wildfowl. Not only had Professor Seal flown in with an assistant from Minnesota; a pig-tailed aviculturist from Hawaii, Dr Fern Duvall, had come over by courtesy of British Airways, and Slimbridge itself fielded a strong team to back them up.

Throughout their deliberations, the English colony of Nenes, 200 strong, was parading about outside as if it owned the place. The birds, tamer than chickens, stump around the buildings in pairs, in and out the picnic tables, ignoring the human hordes and chatting to each other in companionable little droning noises (perhaps the phonetic origin of their name).

Jeff Black knows the species so well that he can interpret every sound. 'He's calling to her to come on and follow him . . . If he didn't expect an answer, he'd be talking more quietly . . .'

In purely avian terms, that is no doubt a correct interpretation. But it is easy for a newcomer, taken with the sheer charm of the Nenes, to imagine that they are lobbying their human benefactors with the simple but ultimate request, 'Save Our Souls'.

Honeymoon Special

Our daughter's wedding went off miraculously well, not least because we were blessed with a day such as we had scarcely dared to hope for: a meteorological masterpiece not foreseen by M. Fish, who had worried us sick by predicting outbreaks of rain.

Dawn came up diamond-bright, with a cool east wind to temper the heat — an ideal combination for every stage of our festivities. One special consideration made us extra-keen to have a fine day. I did not mention it to many people, for fear of provoking the fates; but for the bride and bride-groom's getaway transport, we had laid on a hot-air balloon.

No other facet of our planning worried me half as much as this device, since its success or failure lay beyond our control: for a successful take-off we needed a fine, still evening. I steeled myself, and the bride, to accept the fact that we almost certainly would not get one.

All day, before and after the service, we kept watch on what Highland deer-stalkers call 'the carry' — the direction of cloud-movement. Comfortable as it felt at ground level, the morning's east wind was definitely unwelcome for aeronautical purposes, as it would carry a balloon towards or over the Severn.

Gradually, however, the wind went round, and by afternoon it was back in its usual quarter, the south-west. At 6 pm, with the reception in full swing, it seemed possible that a miracle might be about to occur. Radiant day had softened into golden evening; apart from occasional gusts, the breeze was steadily falling.

In a very short speech I told our guests about the balloon. Loud cheers arose. I begged the multitude to will the wind to die. 'But where will they land?' asked one old lady. 'We've no idea,' I said. 'That's half the point.'

Hardly had I finished when I saw the balloon van drive up the field. I went across. Pete, the pilot, thought the omens looked good. His launch-crew of three began to lay out their red-and-yellow monster on the grass. By then the wind was almost due south. I suggested a 7 pm take-off and warned the bride that she should soon go to change.

As the canopy began to inflate, it heaved and flopped about the field like a dying dinosaur. A long row of spectators, lining the wooden rails of the paddock, could easily have been punters at a race-course. Other guests streamed out into the field itself. As they had by then lowered some 130 bottles of champagne and seventy-odd pints of beer, to say nothing of mountains of very good food, they were in the mood for a spectacular send-off.

They got one. As soon as the honeymoon couple appeared in their going-away clothes, Pete ignited his main burner. Girls screamed and clutched their neighbours as fire roared into the belly of the giant. Two of the launch team, wearing thick gloves, held the mouth of the balloon open to stop the flames singeing it. Quickly the whole loose envelope tautened and came upright.

Confetti and tears flew. 'Get him to lift her into the basket,' cried the photographer from the local newspaper. We relayed the request, but it proved impossible to fulfil, for the sides of the gondola were too high, and the whole contraption had become too frisky. Bride and bridegroom scrambled aboard as decorously as they could. About 25,000 photographs were taken.

Another few blasts of fire had the balloon hopping clear of the ground — but still it was tethered to the van, and held down by the two assistants. After a few last adjustments, Pete snapped the tether free.

A huge cheer seemed to waft the balloon on its way. Then in sudden silence it lifted over the field, over the house, over the valley. After so much twitching and jerking, the smoothness of its ascent was bewitching. Its red and yellow panels blazed in the setting sun. Shouts of farewell rang from high and low as it climbed through the clear evening air towards the woods on the hill. All too soon it diminished to toy-size, and in a few minutes it sailed over the northern horizon, exactly as, for weeks, I had been hoping it would.

Did anyone remain unmoved? All agreed that they had never seen a more romantic departure. The spectacle put people in such ebullient form that nobody noticed the recovery convoy slip away. The van led, followed by my son driving the honeymooners' car, followed by the best man in his own car (to bring my son back). Twisting northward through lanes, they lost sight of the balloon for a few miles, but then picked it up again and kept it in view.

The aeronauts, meanwhile, were having the flight of their lives. The wind took them straight over Woodchester Park, the unfinished Victorian mansion deep in a wooded valley, with five lakes stretching below it. Next they floated up the line of the Cotswold escarpment, whose every ridge and hollow was etched by the brilliant low light. To their left lay the Severn estuary, beyond it the Forest of Dean, beyond that the mountains of Central Wales.

Soon they were over Stroud, where they descended almost to roof-top height and exchanged the time of day with citizens of that town. Then they climbed again to clear the next range of hills just west of Painswick.

After an hour of pure magic the pilot decided to land; but he had to abort his first attempt, as a man seemed to be making menacing gestures from the field at which he had aimed. Climbing briefly again, he clipped the tops of some tall poplars with the basket and plopped down on to a rugger field alongside the main industrial estate on the eastern outskirts of Gloucester.

The basket was dragged for a few yards on its side, but the occupants came to rest none the worse; and the fact that they had to summon a security guard to release them from the sports club's grounds in no way punctured their euphoria. If they had not exactly been round the world in eighty days, at least they had a cut a terrific dash in the first hour or two of their married lives.

★   ★   ★

At the farm, it was most satisfactory to see how our animals and birds made themselves scarce during the reception. 'Where are the peacocks?' people kept asking — and the answer was that they had quietly absented themselves for the duration. When the noisy humans left, they reappeared, having spent a peaceful day in the overgrown spinney next door.

The cats did a similar vanishing act, and even Agamemnon the ram decided to have nothing to do with the party. I had fully expected him at least to put in a token demonstration of fence-smashing, but no — he skulked as far away as possible.

Only the hens continued to go about their business in the outer farmyard, into which revellers could look down. 'Good heavens! Chickens!' cried one man. 'How extraordinary!' I agreed that what he could see was a flock of domestic fowl; but why he found them so irregular, I could not divine — and I don't think he could either.

Next day, the tents came down, everything returned to normal, and from the look of the garden, the wedding might never have happened. As in Francis Bacon's famous remark about the Spanish Armada: 'This great preparation . . . passed away like a dream.' But the old sage was referring to a nightmare, and ours was a dream of glorious fulfilment.

Curse of the Highlands

Anyone who takes to the great outdoors for a holiday between now and October is certain to be tormented by that curse of moor and mountain: midges. Ubiquitous, multitudinous, infuriating, the tiny insects infest rough, wet ground particularly, and nowhere with greater intensity than the Western Highlands of Scotland.

Every hiker, climber, camper, fisherman and deer-stalker knows all too well how, the moment one stops moving, they rise in clouds from heather or peat-hag to feast upon the human interloper, and attack with such persistence that any intricate activity — for instance the unravelling of a snarled-up fishing line — becomes impossible. Even in cultivated woods, fields and gardens they can be a menace, especially at sundown.

I once asked a Highland stalker how long midges live, and long summers of irritation burst out in his two-word answer, enunciated with explosive emphasis: 'TOO LORNG!' Yet his *retort also* indicated complete ignorance about the pest that had plagued him throughout his working life.

Far from being an exclusively Scottish or English nuisance, midges are a worldwide plague. More than 1,000 species exist; in Africa they transmit disease, and in places like Florida, which depend heavily on the tourist trade, millions of dollars are spent annually on attempts to suppress them, mainly by draining and spraying.

In western Scotland alone there are fifty species, many of them non-biting; but the midges that annoy humans are the *Culicoides* — a family of the *Ceratopogonidae,* and the only ones that feed on mammals. The infamous Highland midge is *Culicoides impunctatus* — a name which refers to the light and dark patterns on its wings.

Such information may seem of little consequence to the harassed hiker, sweating, swatting, itching, rubbing and cursing as he tries to read his map through a cloud of incoming attackers. But I myself have often wondered what the little brutes are *doing* throughout the long hours and days when no human comes their way.

The answer — supplied by Dr Richard Lane, an expert at the London School of Hygiene and Tropical Medicine — is that they are lurking in the vegetation near the ground, or in the peat itself. As in other spheres, the female of the species is more deadly than the male, for it is only she who bites.

Whereas the male has practically no jaws, the female must have a feed of fresh blood before she can lay each clutch of fifty to a hundred eggs; and so, every two or three days throughout her life of a couple of weeks, she gets stuck into a rabbit, sheep, cow, deer, human being or bird. Some species feed only on birds, crawling sideways into their feathers.

The female midge's jaw consists of three different pairs of biting, gripping and sucking organs. Being what is known as a pool-feeder, she makes a hole in the skin, in which a tiny pool of blood collects. The agent which makes the bite irritate is the anti-coagulant in her saliva.

People, being short of hair and feathers, offer a prime target — and it is the midge's characteristic habit of landing and crawling that makes the fringes of one's hair and the cuffs of one's jacket favourite areas for infiltration.

The eggs are so small that they can only just be seen with the naked eye when set out on white paper in a laboratory. In the wild, they are laid in wet mud, peat or other choice hosts such as cowpats, and hatch into larvae, which travel through water with wriggling, snake-like movements. Adults are killed by the frosts of late autumn, but their descendants survive the winter as mature larvae buried in the soil: it is thought that their bodies contain some natural anti-freeze, and in any case, as the weather grows colder, they burrow deeper for better protection. In the spring they hatch out.

Although so small, midges are extraordinarily complex organisms, with hundreds of tiny receptors all over their bodies for measuring light, temperature, carbon-dioxide levels and so on. 'Under a microscope, they're really elegant little things,' says Dr Lane enthusiastically. 'They make space-craft look clumsy.'

As everybody who has suffered from them must have noticed, their activities are essentially crepuscular: they fly mainly at dawn and dusk, and on days that are muggy and overcast. In bright sunlight they do not come out at all; nor do they take to the air if the wind-speed is over 4 mph.

It is their intricate sensory equipment that enables them to judge conditions (and smell humans) so well. Yet it is also this equipment that gives humans a chance to keep them at bay. The various repellents on the market — Shoo, Jungle Formula, Mijex — are all based on one or other of the chemicals DMP and DEET, which function not by confronting the insect with something unpleasant, but by confusing its receptors and in effect jamming its radar as it is coming in to land.

The repellents all work pretty well — and it is good to see that Shoo, invented by a Scotsman, Dr William Cumming, more than twenty years ago, but not brought on to the market by his son until the early 1980s, has now gained pole position on the reception desks of many Highland hotels. Smoke also has a deterrent effect, though no one seems sure why. The best defence of all is said to be a special jacket, with a hood, made of half-inch mesh, like a giant string vest, impregnated with one of the chemicals.

For the foreseeable future such ad-hoc protection looks likely to remain man's only means of combat. Various reports have concluded that there is no viable means, biological or chemical, of destroying midges on a big scale.

Although birds and other insects do prey on them, there are so many millions that only a fraction of the population can be eaten; and although they can be killed by insecticide, it would be necessary to spray most of the Highlands every few weeks to make any appreciable difference.

Midges, in other words are here to stay, and the only way to avoid being driven berserk by them is to take to the wilds forearmed.

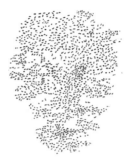

Flight of a Lifetime

Talk about inflation! Not even a South American economy could perform like this. Filled first with cold air, then with hot, our balloon expanded from zero to 77,000 cubic feet in less than a quarter of an hour, until it rose from its prone position on the grass and towered seventy feet above us, its yellow and crimson canopy aflame in the blaze of low sun.

Never can there have been a lovelier evening for a flight: wind soft, air warm, visibility perfect, light spectacular. In fact the air was a bit too warm, and at the last moment our pilot Pete Merrick decided to shed weight by ditching one of his four cylinders of propane gas. With that gone, and only him, myself and my wife on board, the basket began to bob about in lively fashion, held down by the ground crew and tethered to their van.

'Don't touch this red line.' Pete indicated the lanyard running up into the belly of our fragile craft. 'If you pull that, we come down.'

Then he cast off the shackles. Our ascent was smooth as silk. Up we soared, not as I had expected drifting out of the valley at a shallow angle, but rising steeply above our own fields, so that sheep and horses dwindled rapidly to toy size and the house, with its stone outbuildings round the yard, became a child's model of a farm. From somewhere in the garden, Shalimar the peacock sent up a piercing challenge to this bulky invader of his airspace.

As the rim of the basket scarcely reached my hip, I took a few minutes to relax: a glance straight down gave me the feeling that I might at any moment pitch headlong into the void. But there were plenty of struts and rope handles on which to lay hold, and I soon settled down, bewitched by the beauty all around.

The magic of balloon flight lies in its serenity. Even in a glider, one is subject to the pull of gravity forces during turns and harried by the bluster of one's passage through the air. Our nylon envelope, in contrast, floated without the slightest sense of strain. Only the intermittent roar of the burner broke the silence, and for much of the time we cruised as gently as a tuft of thistledown.

If anything, it was warmer aloft than on the ground, for we were travelling at the speed of the wind, and so were effectively in still air. Our heading of north-north-east drew us steadily away from the Cotswold escarpment and up over the hinterland. The views were tremendous, not least to the north-west where, beyond the Severn, the knobbly ridge of the Malvern hills commanded the skyline.

Other aeronauts were taking advantage of that glorious evening. Behind us two more balloons rode high over the southern horizon, a third kept station off to our right, and the pilots of others out of sight popped up now and then on the radio to liaise with their ground crews.

Our own call-sign evoked shades of Waugh and William Boot. There was a certain splendour in the fact that Boot of *The Independent* (if your correspondent may so style himself) was airborne in a contraption called Scoop. But Skylark, Red Leader, Victrix and Jigsaw were all up there somewhere as well. Pete knew the balloons and their pilots, and reported that they all came from Bristol, the centre of hot-air traffic in the south of England.

We, I felt, had an advantage over them in that we were flying above home territory. It was fascinating to look down on the valleys and hills and (more than anything) the houses that we already knew from the ground. Who would have thought that X's roof was in such a state? Had anyone from the council ever set eyes on the ocean of wreckage, rusty corrugated iron, broken machinery and collapsed outbuildings that lapped the back of Y Farm?

Our commanding altitude, reinforced by the low angle of the sun, kept springing surprises: a small lake nestling in a hollow, humps that looked like prehistoric burial mounds, the lines of ancient trackways etched in shadows across the surface of the hills.

Whenever Pete saw cattle, sheep or horses ahead, he climbed higher to avoid disturbing them; but over the villages we drifted low enough for the locals to engage us in conversation. Not all the exchanges were very sensible — 'Are

you part of a race?' 'No — are you?' . . . 'Where are you going?' 'We haven't
a clue' — but all were extremely good-natured. Children capered and turned
cartwheels with excitement. Dogs raced about, barking frenziedly and whirling
their tails.

'Scoop balloon from Scoop retrieve,' came a voice out of the air. 'We've lost
you visual. Can you give us a landmark?'

'We're just about to come off the edge of the map between the zero-four and
the zero-five.'

That seemed to suffice, for a few minutes later we spotted our van heading in
towards our track from the west. But suddenly life became more urgent. The
dream had to break. Shadows were lengthening, colours deepening as the sun
settled towards the horizon. The day was dying about us. Our fuel was running
low. We needed to land.

One fact of travel in a balloon is that you cannot steer. You can climb or
descend, but otherwise you go where the wind takes you. Now the wind was
carrying us over seas of wheat and oilseed rape, with never a grass field in
sight, and Pete was far too professional to countenance a descent into any crop
that he might damage.

We approached a large estate called Miserden, a stretch of country I happen
to know well. 'Can we land in the park?' asked Pete, looking hopefully at a
green splodge on his map. 'Absolutely not,' I told him. 'It's very steep and full
of trees.'

The deep Miserden valley ran north and south across our track, full of
handsome woods. Wanting to land before we came over it, we found nowhere
and were obliged to cross the chasm. Beyond it stretched further seas of rape,
then the village of Winstone.

'There!' said Pete suddenly. 'That little triangular field this side of the
houses. That's grass. I'll go for that.'

The descent was by no means straightforward. Between us and the grass lay
a wood and a line of electricity pylons. 'Don't worry if we touch the trees,'
said Pete. 'Keep your hands inside the basket and take a good hold.'

Down he went, with precision control. We missed the tops of the trees by
three feet, the power lines by six. Suddenly we were plunging towards the
meadow. In the shelter of the wood we descended the last few feet almost
vertically.

Bump! we went, and immediately took off again. *Bump, bump, bump* . . . four
landings for the price of one. Although the basket tilted, it never went over on
its side. By inspired navigation through the lanes, our recovery team had
reached the field first and were waiting to receive us; with their help we
frogmarched the balloon, still upright, to the gate, so there was no need for the
van to drive into the field.

The farm manager's family came out to see the fun. We toasted our safe arrival with glasses of wine, dismantled the balloon and packed it away.

Looking about us, we realised that the sun had set. The western sky had flared into a stunning array of salmon and turquoise bars. We had flown for only eighty minutes and covered no more than a dozen miles; but as we piled into the van and trundled home we felt we were returning from the flight of a lifetime.

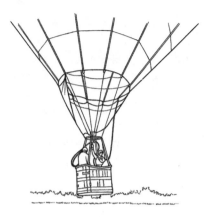

September

Raiding the Bees

In my view the only sensible course of action over a bank holiday weekend is to stay put and avoid driving anywhere. We did just that — but let no one imagine that we went short of novelty or excitement, for I tackled that most traumatic of annual tasks, the taking of the honey.

No matter how often this comes round, it remains — for the amateur apiarist — a test of nerve. Physically, you are in some danger of being stung; and, quite apart from that, you are on thin ice morally, for you are treacherously rounding on the bees, which you have treated in friendly fashion for the rest of the year, and stealing most of their stocks laid in for the winter.

Unlike some other operations, removing the honey involves doing physical violence to the hive, as its lifts, or storeys (which the bees have carefully glued together) must be prized apart, with the result that the inner sanctum of the colony is suddenly exposed to the air. No wonder the inhabitants resent it.

One of my hives contains dark, Italian bees, which are exceptionally aggressive. So firmly were their lifts stuck together that I could not help shaking the whole edifice about when I went to separate them.

Out came the defenders, attacking by the hundred — and instinct directed them unerringly towards the most vulnerable spots on the human aggressor. Dozens bombed into my veil, aiming for my eyes, and others lined up in fours and fives, shoulder to shoulder, battling to penetrate the elasticated cuffs of my gloves.

Safe inside my protective suit, I made off unscathed. Not so my neighbour, who was innocently mowing his grass the other side of a high hedge. Twice that evening, and twice the next, he was stung by infuriated scouts on the look-out for targets of opportunity. Probably it was the hum of his machine which provoked the assaults — for bees hate vibration. Certainly his miniature tractor cut some unusual shapes in the sward when the attacks went home, and he himself — as Old Bill the gardener used to say — took off out of the driving seat 'a bit lissom'.

As I carried the lifts away, I could feel from the weight that they contained a lot of honey. What I could not tell, before I took out the combs, was what sort of honey I had got.

Until this year we have been blessedly out of range of that menace oil-seed rape. This time, however, a field of it was grown on the rim of the valley less than a mile away, and I greatly feared that much of our honey must have come from the flowers which blazed there in early summer. Rape honey is fine if taken off within a few days of being made; but if you miss that moment at the end of May or the beginning of June — as I did this year — it goes so hard as to be unshiftable by any normal means and becomes practically useless, except to hand back to the bees as food for the winter.

Sure enough: whole combs, instead of having a mottled look beneath their wax capping, were pasty white all over, and contained a solid mass with the consistency of the icing on a superannuated Christmas cake. Others, luckily, had been filled before or after the rape came into flower, and so were normal.

There was also one mystery lift, which came from a hive which I took over during the winter. The previous owner had not touched it at all for a year or more, so that the honey in it was at least twelve months old, possibly twenty-four.

The combs looked extraordinary — thick, corrugated and almost black, as if they had been put aside in an Egyptian tomb to see some Pharaoh through the after-life. But when I sliced off the capping with a hot knife, beautiful, liquid honey began to drip out, and I swiftly got the combs into the extractor, to add their contents to the general blend.

The result is honey with a wonderful deep amber colour, and an immensely powerful taste — not of lime or clover or any single species, but an ineffable amalgamation of the scents of summer. The satisfaction of having the larder full of it is not easily described, even if we got no more than half the total.

★   ★   ★

Throughout the taking and extracting and potting of it, I kept thinking of a scene which I witnessed a few weeks ago in the Caucasus. We were driving up a phenomenal canyon which led from the Black Sea into the mountains. Rock walls 1,500 feet high towered vertically on either hand, and down the chasm, which would have tickled the fancy of Kubla Khan, boiled a torrent of melted glacier-water so brilliantly blue-green that no artist would have dared render its colour accurately.

Here and there, in little clearings among the trees on the valley floor, stood groups of beehives — small, battered-looking hutches bearing traces of pink, yellow or blue paint. Suddenly from the back of the bus our guide gave a shout, and the driver pulled violently into a layby.

We walked a few yards down a path through the trees and came to a sunny clearing, which contained a cluster of about twenty hives. At one side stood a couple of wooden huts, with a table set out between them beneath an awning of old canvas.

A honey stall? Yes: plates spread about the table contained fresh, clear, runny honey — this year's vintage, just taken. The family in charge were offering torn-up hunks of white bread to dip in it, for tasting.

The air was absolutely whizzing with bees, and the plates were crawling with them, some already half-drowned, others fully alert, so that dipping had to be done with circumspection. The bread was home-made and delicious, with a smoky tang on the crust which suggested that it had just been baked in an outdoor oven. The honey — to my tongue — rather lacked character: like the bread, it was admirably fresh, but it seemed to have little taste, and was like sugar-syrup.

In spite of this, other passers-by were bearing off pots of it as though it was liquid gold — and that, in fact, would be no bad description, for the price was appalling — 10 roubles a pound, or about £7.50 at the official rate of exchange. Yet, considering that no honey was available in the shops, the hunger for it was hardly surprising.

Then, as I tasted and assessed, I became aware that something else was going on as well. A man nudged my elbow and put into my hand a glass containing what I thought was water. One sniff disillusioned me: a taste nearly blew my head off. It was home-brewed vodka of shattering strength. The little encampment, far from being a mere apiary, was also a shebeen.

'Very good with honey!' said my neighbour enthusiastically. I sipped. I gasped. I blinked. '*Ochen horosho*!' I croaked.

The effect of bread-and-honey chased by firewater was instant incandescence, nectar aflame. After a few experiments, there was nothing for it but to plunge hands and face into the river, whose water, coming straight from the ice-fields 5,000 feet above us, was breathtakingly cold. Our companions from Moscow, where vodka is rationed, and coupons are needed to buy even the two half-litres allowed per head per month, bought all the bottles they could carry, and we went on our way clinking, a good deal merrier.

The inevitable result is that I now associate beehives with you-know-what, and I am wondering whether, for a shebeen discreetly sited in the hedge between me and my neighbour, planning permission would be required.

The Nippiest Whippets

You could hear the noise from several fields away: a non-stop cacophony of yelps and yaps, whimpers and whines, with an undertone of grinding and groaning, the whole in fifty different sharps and flats, punctuated by the odd stentorian roar of a human voice, usually female, and occasional tinny announcements over a loudspeaker.

Connoisseurs could have told with their eyes shut that whippet racing was in progress — and indeed on the sports ground in the village of Nympsfield an open meeting of the South Cotswolds Whippet Racing Club was in full cry. Owners from as far afield as Cornwall, Manchester, Newmarket and Kent had brought no fewer than 142 dogs to compete, purely for the fun of it — for there is no money in this game: no cash prizes, no betting and no skulduggery. It is, as its practitioners claim, an exceptionally clean sport.

In contrast to that other rustic pastime ferret racing — which stirs deep emotions in patrons such as Chas Wright, our friendly neighbourhood brewer — this one moves like lightning. Whereas ferrets may take half an hour to negotiate a ten-yard length of drain-pipe (especially if they go to sleep half-way along it), whippets travel at forty mph and can cover 200 yards in under thirteen seconds.

A race went off just as I arrived. The blue doors of the traps snapped open, and out hurtled four dogs in pursuit of the lure — a tassel of white rag skittering away from them on the end of a wire. One of the runners disgraced herself by veering to the right, bounding high over the opposition and pulling up, but the rest vanished round the left-hand bend towards the finish.

'She's like Desert Orchid!' bayed the lady owner to no one in particular as she recovered the errant bitch. 'Can't go left-handed. I don't know why. Sometimes I think she's got a bad hip and she's running into the pain. Sometimes I think she's just a bloody stupid animal.'

'How do you train them?' I asked — and the answer was that whippets need no education to make them chase things. 'They're sight hounds,' said the lady.

'Chase anything that moves. Leaves, butterflies. Swallows with white tummies, because they're aerial rabbits. This one used to chase helicopters . . .'

Learning to race, I gathered, was another matter. First a dog is allowed to chase the lure for a short distance. Next it is put through an open trap, then through a closed trap; then it is run with one other dog, later, with two, until it shows no sign of 'interfering' — here a technical term, which means turning its head towards its neighbours in play or aggression.

The South Cotswolds WRC was founded five years ago by a group of local enthusiasts, and now is flourishing with thirty-five members, who pay annual subscriptions of £10, meet every Sunday morning and hold two open days a year. At first the club was viewed with some alarm by the villagers of Nympsfield, who feared it would make too much noise and foul up the sports field; but now it has become a fixture, paying an annual rent of £150 and special fees of £20 per open day.

The club chose Nympsfield because of the excellent texture of its ground: the turf is smooth and thick, and retains its spring even in dry weather — a vital requirement for fast-moving dogs whose bones are extremely brittle. The field as a whole lies on a slight slope, and the whippets run uphill, but this is regarded as an advantage, as it tests the competitors' strength.

Most whippet races are held over 150-yard straights or 240-yard courses with a full, ninety-degree bend. Nympsfield is unusual in that the course is a 200-yard half-bend — a length and shape dictated by the size of the field; but because of its good sward it is regarded as one of the best tracks in England.

The proceedings last Sunday gave the agreeable impression of being amateur in the best sense of the term, and at the same time extremely well run. The set of six electrically-operated starting traps, for instance, had been made by one of the members, using solenoids from Lada cars as the motors. The cost — £400 — had been about one-third of that of a professional set.

The mechanism which wound in the lure on the end of a wire was likewise a car starter-motor, and after each of the day's ninety-three races the lure was run out again by a fair-haired boy on a pink scooter. Cars were drawn up all over the field (except on the cricket square), facing into the elbow of the course, with humans in the front and competitors in wire cages in the back. One or two mobile shops were selling essentials like patent tick-remover and vitamin-and-mineral supplements, and in the little pavilion ladies from the village were dispensing excellent teas — a labour of love which earned some £100 for church funds.

The sun blazed down, the breeze was cool, and there was none of the sleaze or shiftiness associated with greyhound racing: people had simply come to enjoy themselves. All agreed that you cannot do much to make a whippet go faster: you feed it correctly and walk it three or four miles a day, but beyond that almost everything rests on natural ability. Another vital factor is weight, for competitors are divided into four narrow bands — 15–19lb, 20–22lb, 23–25lb and 27–30lb — and handicaps in favour of the lighter dogs range between eighteen inches and a yard per pound.

Heats, semi-finals and finals are run off in each group, and then, as the climax of the meeting, comes the Supreme, in which the winners from each weight race each other. Here the lightweights usually have an unassailable advantage: no matter how big or powerful a heavyweight, it cannot make up ten or eleven yards in so short a sprint.

Consider Agile Dreamer, the champion bitch bred by and belonging to Steve Bryant, who works for the Prudential in Reading. She turns the scales at only 18lb. Her ribs show, as they should, but down her back and loins runs a tremendous ridge of muscle. Last year she won almost all her fifty races. As her owner says, 'She's real nippy. She's out of the trap and away, and they can't catch her. Then at the end of a race she's so happy she dances all over the place.'

This natural racing machine breakfasts off Weetabix and milk or scrambled egg, and has her main meal of mince and patent biscuit-mix at tea-time. On racing days she has breakfast earlier than usual, and between races is sustained by sips of milky tea with glucose in it.

At home, she lives in the house, like the pet she is, along with her father Agile Mover (another champion) and several other whippets; often in the evenings the Bryant family are obliged to watch television from the floor, the chairs all being occupied by dogs. Like other owners, they travel the length and breadth of the country to race.

On Sunday Agile Dreamer was admirably composed — not shivering with nerves or whining between races, as many of her fellow-competitors were, but waiting calmly, perhaps secure in the knowledge that she had the measure of the opposition.

Sure enough: having romped through all the races at her own weight, she went on to win the Supreme by a distance, top dog yet again; and the exuberance of her victory dance seemed to sum up the good-natured spirit of the whole meeting. It may be true that only mad dogs and Englishmen go out in the midday sun — but when they do, they certainly make the best of it.

Stone-Walling

We took many a deep breath before tackling the dry-stone walls that separate farmyard and garden, because we knew that to rebuild them would be an expensive job. Yet there came a moment when we could stand the sight of them no longer: leaning in all directions, sprouting weeds, collapsing at points where frost had burst the stone, they lowered the tone of the place intolerably.

Enter Leslie, an admirable local stone-mason. I knew from previous experience that he likes to be on the safe side. Even so, the quantities of material which he prescribed seemed prodigious: 500 eighteen-by-nine-by-nine hollows (concrete blocks for the backing walls, out of sight against the banks), eleven tons of aggregate (for concrete foundations), seven tons of sand (for muck, as mortar is called hereabouts) and twenty tons of stone for the walls proper.

My first step was to find a home for the rubble which the reconstruction would throw up; and by a great stroke of luck, it turned out that our neighbour half a mile down the lane was wanting hardcore to raise the level of his farmyard. Still better, he lent me a six-ton tipping trailer.

At eight on the appointed morning, Leslie arrived with his assistant, Pat, diminutive but wiry. Our first task was to dismantle the old walls — and all three of us pitched in with hands, crowbars and pickaxes.

To me, at first, one chunk of stone was much like another. 'Hang on to that!' cried Leslie (a stickler for conservation in its most literal sense) as I was about to pitch an ugly lump into the trailer. 'Don't throw out anything that's any good.' Soon I was beginning to distinguish between 'rubbish', which was no good for anything, and 'stone', which had at least one presentable face and could be used again.

A few old artefacts came to light, but nothing that gave a clue as to when the walls had been built. Yet the rotten mortar was full of woodlice, which tumbled out sleepily as we burrowed away; and it also contained bigger game. At one moment, with a sudden yell, Pat leapt back across the yard. Urgent inquiries revealed that he had touched a toad, which sat there looking slightly dishevelled. 'Didn't that give I a fright!' he groaned. 'I hates they!'

With the trailer full, I set out for the tip, my short drive enlivened by the fact that the tractor's front wheels were almost airborne from the weight on the tow-bar, and that, whenever I touched the brakes, the whole *equipe* took a sharp pace to the left.

So a pattern was set: day after day of excavation, trip after trip down the lane. It was back-breaking work, at which my two henchmen stuck with astonishing persistence and stamina. The sheer weight of stone was colossal: I reckon we took away fifty tons of rubbish, and saved perhaps forty tons of good stone, among which were lumps, prized from the old foundations, weighing four or five hundredweight apiece.

In went new foundations — eight inches of concrete — and up went the block walls, beautifully straight and level. I hardly need relate that the first load of sand — a ton, got by me — turned out to be rubbish. 'Horrible stuff,' Leslie pronounced. 'I couldn't build anything with that — only something that's going to be out of sight.'

The rotten sand sufficed for the block walls. Then a seven-ton load of proper stuff arrived, beautifully fine and grey, and perfect for creamy muck. Meanwhile, however, a crisis was brewing, for we were being let down again and again by contractors who promised to deliver the walling stone.

Fast operators, still faster talkers, they were buying up old buildings or obsolete field-walls and flogging off the stone at £40 a ton. Soon I perceived that their excuses were all uncannily similar: the lorry had broken down, the land was too wet for heavy vehicles, the farmer wouldn't let aliens on the place during the harvest . . .

Almost all this was nonsense. The truth was that the contractors were in a frenzy, frantically pursuing ever-bigger deals, and not interested in a small fish like me. We got a revealing glimpse of their real world when one of them invited us to look at a derelict farm he was about to demolish, and see if the stone there suited us.

Leslie, I hardly need say, pronounced it to be rubbish — the wrong colour, and too thick — but in any case, the place was in chaos, for when our contractor had arrived that morning (he told us) he had found cowboys already stripping a barn roof of tiles, and had called in the Law.

At last we got some stone, and the real walls began to go up. We had already decided, for aesthetic reasons, that one of them could be built with muck; but the rest are dry stone, and, as Leslie explained, the degree of perfection in the finish is directly related to the amount of money one is prepared to lay out.

Given unlimited funds, he could spend minutes or even hours searching for precisely the right piece of stone for every next slot, and so make the walls a work of art. Even with a compromise struck between expense and expediency, I should say they are that anyway, so skilled and meticulous is he.

The job is by no means finished, but it will look wonderful when it is done, and in the meantime I have learned a good deal, not least how to trim a lump of stone with a hammer, and how to tell by the ring whether or not it is flawed. I also inserted, into a concrete block filled with more concrete, a small time capsule containing a note about myself, my family and the state of the parish in 1988, together with some coins and other contemporary trivia.

Given the massive strength of Leslie's construction, it is on the cards that the capsule will be there for eternity, or anyway for several centuries: as he remarked while he watched me secreting it, 'Anybody'd have to hit into the wall fairish, if they're ever going to see that thing again.'

Lady with Birds and Badgers

'You should have been here yesterday,' the artist Eileen Soper once wrote to a friend. 'I walked out into the garden with milled cheese on top of my head! Several long-tailed tits perched there feeding . . .'

It is a curious experience to be let loose among the papers of someone recently dead, especially if the person concerned was manifestly eccentric. With every new box opened, every packet undone, you feel you are about to come on the one document which will reveal all.

When the watercolours and drawings of Eileen Soper go on sale at the Wildlife Art Gallery in Lavenham tomorrow, everyone present will see what talent she had, and what devotion went into her pictures of badgers, foxes, deer, hedgehogs, birds and other wild creatures. But nobody will be able to divine from her art what it was that spurred her to such efforts — what made her, for instance, devote over 500 hours, most of them nocturnal, to the observation of badgers.

Although I never met her, I knew a good deal about her before I began work on her life last year. She died in March 1990 at the age of eighty-five, and she had lived all her life in the house called Wildings, outside Welwyn, in Hertfordshire.

When she was taken into hospital in the spring of 1989, along with her elder sister Eva, who was almost 90, rescuers found the house in an extraordinary state. The four-acre garden had reached, grown over and almost buried the building; inside, the rooms were jammed to the doorways with piles of newspapers, books, clothes inside plastic bags, and boxes of papers. In the north-facing studio on the first floor was a stunning cache of unframed artwork, partly by the sisters' father George Soper, the distinguished horse-artist, and partly by Eileen herself, conservatively estimated to be worth nearly £1 million.

It was clear that during the past ten years or so the spinsters had gradually lost control of their environment. Like a pair of mice, they had lived happily enough among the tremendous accumulation of belongings — and indeed, from hospital Eileen sent a message asking that the mice which were nesting in her slippers should not be disturbed.

Shortage of money was not the problem. When the old ladies died within a few months of each other, they left £250,000 in cash and securities, to say nothing of the pictures, the house and the extensive garden — itself worth a fortune in stockbroker Hertfordshire. What was it that had made them so reclusive?

The cardboard boxes filled in a good deal about Eileen's life, for they contained an incredible amount of paper. Much of it was of little or no value — bank statements from the 1930s, share-prospectuses from the 1950s, letters from bank managers, receipts; but among all this dross was hundreds of copies of her letters, mainly from 1942 onwards: in that year she acquired a portable typewriter, and kept carbons of everything she wrote.

She and Eva scarcely went to school: they were taught mainly by their father, and learnt everything they knew about art from him. Under George's tuition, Eileen became so proficient that she had two etchings hung at the Royal Academy in 1921, when she was still only 15 — the youngest-ever exhibitor.

From etching she progressed to the illustration of books, and in 1942 joined forces with that volcanic story-teller Enid Blyton, with whom she maintained a profitable partnership for more than twenty years, drawing the pictures for many of the Famous Five adventures.

Not until 1951, when she was forty-six, did she see her first badger. Then, sitting up over a sett at night, she felt 'breathless excitement' and 'a sense of wonder' which she had not experienced for years. Immediately she became a fanatical badger-watcher, and launched out on a new career as an observer, recorder and painter of wildlife. All the watercolours which go on show tomorrow derive from the most productive period of her life, in the 1950s and 1960s.

The documents make it clear that by this time she had become unusual, to say the least, in her devotion to birds and other wild creatures. In one letter she described how, sitting on a garden bench, she allowed great tits to pull out beakfuls of her hair and carry them off for their nests. The birds in her garden were so tame that they would feed from her hand, and often they invaded the house, ripping out the stuffing from sofas and boring holes in the covers of books. Eileen was so soft-hearted that she could not bear to kill any creature, however much it was provoking her, and whenever mice became intolerably audacious, she caught them in box-traps and paid a neighbour to chauffeur them to distant release-points.

All this was good fun, but it did not solve the central mystery of Eileen's increasingly reclusive behaviour. Then came the breakthrough — not from the archive, but from a woman in Hertfordshire, who had seen an appeal of mine for information.

A neighbour and former friend of the Sopers, she divulged the vital secret: that Eileen and Eva had been subjugated by their unreasoning horror of cancer, which they referred to as The Dread Disease. In spite of frequent assurances to the contrary, they believed that cancer could be caught like a common cold, through airborne germs — and the effect of this delusion was incalculable.

It meant, for instance, that they could not — without paralysing anxiety — travel on public transport, go into a shop, eat at a restaurant, or even enter the houses of friends. When old family retainers retired, the sisters did not dare replace them, for fear that a newcomer might bring the Dread Disease into their house.

Suddenly everything made sense. I already knew that George Soper had had an obsession about germs, and that, when his daughters were small, he had forbidden their nanny to allow any stranger near them during their daily walks. When Eileen went down with appendicitis at the age of eighteen, his dread of hospitals was such that he got the gardener to scrub the kitchen table, and had the patient operated on in the studio. Clearly, it was this deep-seated fear of disease which had bred the cancer-phobia.

In many ways the effect of it was pathetic: the sisters shopped mainly by post, rarely entertained and had practically no social life. The older they grew, the more they were confined to their house and wild garden, which — because they were too scared to have anyone helping them — gradually deteriorated into jungle.

Yet I believe that the phobia also had one immensely constructive effect: that of concentrating Eileen's energy and focusing it on her wildlife paintings. Undistracted by the demands of family or friends, she devoted herself to her art in a way that would have been impossible for anyone with normal social obligations.

The result is a spectacular legacy. I feel that in many ways she was a selfish and demanding person, especially when she grew older. But besides her skill and artistic integrity, she had tremendous courage, and for that I salute her.

Sheepish Champion

The sheep seemed not in the least put out by their early start. At 5.25 am four ewes and one ram boarded the trailer with minimal fuss, and a few minutes later we were grinding uphill out of the valley, en route for Northampton, 100 miles to the north-east.

It was a long way to go on the off-chance of selling five sheep; but for us this was no ordinary occasion. Our chosen breed, Wiltshire Horn, has only two specialist sales a year — one at Northampton and one still farther off, in Anglesey — and for anybody who wants to buy or sell pedigree animals, attendance at one or other gathering is essential. Our aim was to get rid of all five animals, if possible, and to buy a new ram.

An easy three-hour drive brought us to the showground — a golf-course on the outskirts of the town. Arriving in a downpour, we found sheep being assembled for the main sale by the thousand: great droves of them were swirling and seething about. But the number of Wiltshire Horns was mercifully small, and we discovered that we had a cosy little section of pens made from traditional wooden hurdles.

The rain soon eased off, and owners began to preen their animals for the judging. Most of the sheep had already been shampooed, but even the snowiest got a last-minute brushing and smoothing. Our ewes seemed bigger than most — were they too fat? — and Domingo, our shearling ram, named because of his ringing tenor voice, looked long and well-built in comparison with his rivals. (A shearling is a second-year animal, from fifteen to eighteen months old.)

The judge was a spare, elderly farmer with an impassive, weatherbeaten face. As each class went into the ring, and he walked round and round them, it was impossible to tell what he was thinking. Then he would rearrange the competitors, asking one of the handlers to move a particular animal to the end of the line. Next he would shift another, shuffling and reshuffling the sheep like a hand of cards until satisfied that he had them in the right order.

Our ewes came nowhere. So little time did the judge have for them that they finished bottom of the line — but as we took them out of the ring, some friendly stranger murmured words of consolation. 'Lovely sheep,' he said. 'Dunno what came over him. I thought he was judging from the other end.'

When Domingo's turn came, things were very different. To our amazement, he won not only the class for shearling rams but also the breed championship, beating all comers in the final. Suddenly my wife, who is boss in these matters, found herself with a tricolor rosette, a cup and the congratulations of the multitude.

That would have been excitement enough. But immediately after the judging, the sale began. An auctioneer in a white coat mounted a raised, pulpit-like rostrum at one side of the ring, and through a loud-hailer entered into vociferous competition with two other salesmen soliciting offers from other rings close by.

Just as bidding began, a class of schoolchildren arrived, doing a project on sheep. With small faces peering over the hurdles, they looked considerably bewildered, and I did not blame them, for things started happening very fast.

'Do I hear seventy guineas?' our man rattled out. 'Seventy guineas. Seventy. Sixty, then. Come on, gentlemen. He's brought them here to sell them, not to take them away. What's sixty guineas for a fine shearling ewe? She'll do you well. She can only improve. Sixty guineas. No? Fifty, then. Thank you, Madam. Fifty guineas. Two. Four. Six. Eight. Fifty eight and out the gate? No. Sixty. Two. Four . . .'

Soon it became clear that most people were buying as well as selling; in effect, they were swapping sheep among themselves to change their flocks' bloodlines. Yet at the same time, they demonstrated their disagreement with the judge by bidding at variance with his placings.

First we got another welcome boost when all four of our ewes — officially deemed to be of no merit — sold quickly and well, the best for eighty guineas. But then came a heavy put-down. When Domingo entered the ring, loudly cracked up as the champion of the day, nobody bid at all. Humiliation threatened. What was the matter? Was he too long, too big, too docile?

At last, to our unbounded relief, somebody bid ninety guineas, and my wife made a somewhat crestfallen exit from the ring. To ease our disappointment, we bought a ram lamb named John, who had come second in his class, for 100 guineas.

By lunch-time we were on our way home, emotionally drained by the ups and downs of the morning, but £300-odd better off, and with a fine newcomer to take charge of our flock. My lasting memory is of the friendliness of our rival owners. Never mind the sheep: it was worth going all that way to meet the people who breed them.

★ ★ ★

Meanwhile, the season of mists and mellow fruitfulness has come and almost gone. When rain at last fell after that glorious burst of Indian summer in September, we thought we might find the fields carpeted with mushrooms — but no such luck. Although we have picked a few, we never got a downpour hard enough to precipitate a real uprising.

On the other hand, those harbingers of autumn, puffballs, flourished mightily. For several weeks the fanciers were out in force, hackles up, eyes alight, as they coursed about in search of the huge white golfballs which gleamed from the grass fields on the sides of the valley. In our part of the world puffballs seem to favour elevated positions, close under the woods which hang on the escarpment, and big ones — a foot or more in diameter — can be seen from at least half a mile away.

For me, a puffball is scarcely worth eating, as it has practically no taste. A slice fried in bacon fat is good enough — but only because it tastes of bacon, with a hint of mushroom in the background. Yet connoisseurs pursue them fanatically — and even I am bound to admit that there is something fascinating about their texture.

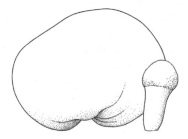

A good specimen, at the prime of its short life, emits a rich thump, suggestive of moisture under tension, when tapped with one's knuckles, and its flawless white flesh yields beautifully smooth, even slices when carved with a sharp knife.

A puffball also explodes with a most satisfactory splatter if shot with a full-bore rifle bullet; yet later in life it achieves a surprising toughness. The other day I drove over two yellowing monsters with the tractor-mounted hay-cutter, and instead of being chopped to bits by the blades, they flew out of the machine intact, travelling horizontally at high speed like well-struck footballs.

Sometimes even a seasoned hunter can be led astray. One morning I spotted five shining white blobs, in two groups, three and two, away on the far side of the stream. The field was slightly too close for comfort to a farm belonging to brothers of uncertain temper, but a footpath ran down one side of it, and a small detour would surely harm nobody . . .

After a circuitous approach along the hedges, I reached the field and moved stealthily upwards. Now . . . this was about where they were. No sign of them. In a hollow, then? There *was* no hollow. Nor were there any puffballs. By then the five white blobs had upped and flown, roosting seagulls every one.

October

Claret tames the Wild

'The old house'll talk to you tonight,' said the stalker cheerfully. Then he was gone, away down the loch in his boat, and I was left alone in the heart of the wilderness, seven miles from the nearest human settlement, with dusk coming down and the wind rising.

I had only half anticipated this. 'We'll send you off to one of the outlying lodges,' my host had said when, with magnificent generosity, he invited me to go deer-stalking in the north-west Highlands. Yet somehow I had expected to be accompanied by at least one other guest.

The grey house stood hunched against the foot of a mountain. Behind it, on the steep grass slopes which ran up to vertical cliffs, stags were roaring defiance at one another as they jealously shepherded their hinds. In front, five stout Garron ponies — three white, two dun — grazed in a bare paddock, tails to the wind. Otherwise no living thing moved in that colossal expanse of rough grass, heather, rock and water.

In country as big as that, you can see the weather coming from miles away. As I stood taking stock, a grey curtain of rain swept in across the glen from the south and blotted out the black mountain-face across the loch. It was time to go indoors.

I had forgotten how different life is without electricity. Inside the lodge, the dregs of daylight drained away into the dark pine panelling of walls and ceiling, into the bare wood floor, into the dresser against the kitchen wall. The little room was full of such deep shadows that I could not even find a match to light one of the oil lamps.

After eight hours' scrambling about the hills, I was glad to sit down in front of the Rayburn stove and take my boots off as I considered my next move. I should start preparations for supper — peel some potatoes, get them on to boil. Instead, I just sat . . . and began to worry.

Night fell. The wind rose to a full gale. Bursts of rain rattled on the windows, interspersed by sharper volleys of hail. The house did indeed begin to talk: the chimneys boomed and roared, the panelling started to click and creak. Wind thundered and drummed in the roof. The kettle on the stove suddenly gave a squealing noise which my imagination had no difficulty in interpreting as a distant human scream.

I began to hear other noises: an engine outside (impossible, because there was no road within miles), the bark of a dog (equally impossible). Then, in a lull between gusts, I did hear the scrape and clink of horseshoes as one of the ponies came to the fence outside the door.

My nerves had grown taut. But what was I scared of? Not of ghosts, because I did not feel that the place was haunted. Not of the mice for which dishes of poison had been set out at strategic points around the house. I was not afraid that a homicidal maniac would break in on me, as in some yarn by Sapper, nor yet that a Baskerville-type hound would materialise out of the howling darkness. After all, I had a .300 magnum at my elbow.

No — it was none of these things. What was disconcerting me (I began to realise after a while) was the unaccustomed isolation, the sudden severance from all the everyday adjuncts of modern life which one normally takes for granted. I could not flick a switch to dispel the darkness with bright lights. There was no telephone on which I might talk to someone miles away. There was no radio — still less a television set — to conjure voices, faces or music out of the air. In short, I had no means of communicating with, or even hearing, any other human being.

Why should that matter, for one wild autumn night? It was hard to say. But as the gale roared and the house shuddered beneath its impact, I found myself fighting down feelings of claustrophobia, almost of panic.

There was one easy way to escape the sensation of being hemmed in: go outside. I tried it once — and in a few seconds I was back indoors, dripping and almost blown off my feet.

Yet that one blast brought me to my senses. A hundred years ago (it struck me abruptly), *everyone* lived like this. Before the universal spread of electricity, every household was isolated at night, and cut off from communication as a matter of routine.

Action was the obvious cure for anxiety. With an effort, I got moving. Finding a box of matches, I lit several oil-lamps and stationed them about the kitchen. I lit the fire of wood and coal in the sitting room and put the guard in front of it.

With a candle to guide me, I padded along to the storeroom in stockinged feet and fetched some potatoes from a sack on the floor. In the gas-powered fridge I found a pack of bacon — good for a main course. A cupboard well stocked with tins furnished plenty of other ideas: game soup for a starter, fruit salad for pudding.

Then I remembered the wine. In the cupboard under the stairs (my host had told me) I would find some 'fairly decent claret'. That proved the

understatement of the century. As my torch-beam picked out the labels —
Chateau La Lagune, Chateau Palmer, Chateau Pichou Lalande — I could
scarcely believe my eyes. Mastering my incredulity, I chose a bottle of Chateau
Brane Cantenac (whose vintage I dare not relate), opened it and set it to breathe
on the shelf above the stove.

Cooking by lamp and candlelight is a chancy business: you cannot see down
into saucepans, especially when steam is rising from them, and much has to be
done by touch. Besides, in a strange and ill-lit kitchen, you spend an
extraordinary amount of time simply walking about in search of things.
Notwithstanding these hazards, I eventually had potatoes coming to the boil,
diced bacon sizzling gently in a frying-pan, and tinned tomatoes warming on
another hob.

A bath seemed the next logical step. The old-fashioned tub was very short —
little more than a hip-bath — but the water was scalding hot, and a candlelit
wallow proved exceedingly relaxing. By the end of it my confidence was so
well restored that the howl of the wind and the shadows leaping about the walls
held no menace whatever.

And so, clad in a warm, dry tracksuit, I addressed myself to my solitary
dinner. The food on its own might not have won a medal; but given my hunger,
and the majestic wine, the meal became a banquet fit for a king.

By setting three lamps in a ring on the table, I made a pool of light bright
enough to read by, and so I ate and drank with my back to the night and my
mind far away on board Conrad's *Narcissus* during her fateful passage from
Bombay to London.

Come nine o'clock, I felt replete, and too sleepy to read any more. The fire
in the sitting-room had gone out. Early as it was, I left the dishes unwashed,
doused the lamps, and went up the narrow, twisting staircase of bare boards to
bed.

In spite of Wagnerian noises off, I slept like a stone. When I woke at 7 am,
the storm was so violent that many of the burns, instead of tumbling in
waterfalls as they came over rock-ledges, were being blown skywards in sheets
of whirling white spray.

Even so, I felt a great sense of peace. Perhaps it was simply that I had adjusted to solitude. Perhaps it was the claret which had done the trick. Whatever the cause, I felt entirely at home, and positively looked forward to spending the rest of the week on my own in the wilds.

Lost in the Beddywine

Our neighbour has had a tough time with his cattle lately.

First one of his cows was shot in the middle of the night by a gamekeeper sniping at a fox. The marksman claimed to have had bad luck, in that it was a ricochet which hit the cow; even so, the incident strikingly demonstrated the dangers of using a high-velocity rifle on land frequented by farm animals and humans, especially at night, when one has only a limited idea of what may lie in the background.

Spotting the fox in the beam of his lamp, the gamekeeper fired at it across a small valley. He reckoned the shot was safe enough, because the target was on a steep grass bank, in which he supposed the bullet would come to rest. Yet by evil chance it hit the bottom rail of an old iron fence and flew upwards, catching a cow in the throat.

Daylight found the animal bleeding freely and in a state of shock. The bullet had nicked the skin over her windpipe and gone up into her jaw. The vet, hastily summoned, did what he could, but could not operate immediately, as it was impossible to see where the projectile had come to rest.

For several days the cow's fate remained uncertain. She would not eat or drink, and the farmer was afraid that, at the very least, she would lose the calf she was carrying. Gradually, however, she returned more or less to normal, and this week — a month after the event — the vet did operate, removing five fragments of the bullet, which had finally given its position away by raising a lump on her cheek. That the cow has survived at all seems a miracle: a fractional difference in the trajectory of the ricochet, and she would have been one more unwanted carcass.

Meanwhile, another traumatic saga had begun, this time in a maternity ward well out of the gamekeeper's range. One morning at about 9 am a calf was born in a field, and because all looked well, the farmer left it and its mother alone. That evening, however, he saw the cow kicking the calf away when it tried to suck her; thinking that she must have a sore udder, he decided to bring her into the yard for the night, and, with the help of his wife and younger son, drove cow and calf in just as dusk was falling. At the last moment, however, both animals bolted, and the calf disappeared into the dark.

If the cow had bellowed for her offspring, all might have been well; but she, being a first-time mother, showed no anxiety and remained mute. The result was that the calf stayed out all night.

Walking with my dogs early next morning, unaware that anything was amiss, I met the farmer's elder son searching along a hedgerow. He explained what had happened, and said that the calf was dark-brown, almost chocolate coloured, with no white on it, and therefore difficult to spot. Almost certainly, it was curled up somewhere in the undergrowth: its instinct, like that of a fawn, would be to lie low. The whole family was out looking for it.

The triangular field in which the animal had last been seen lay on the very edge of the escarpment. From it, the calf could have gone in any direction: out into the flat fields on top of the hill, or down into either of two wooded valleys which fell steeply away on the sides of a spur. Topographically speaking, it could not have picked a more challenging point, or one with more complicated possibilities, from which to disappear.

Joining in the search, I changed my projected route and took a swing down through a gully in the woods, hoping that if the dogs scented the fugitive, they would put it up, or at least bark at it. We drew blank, however, and for the rest of the morning I was occupied with other things.

In the afternoon I again found the farmer and his wife out hunting, and although I was really bent on an errand of my own, I felt I must give them a hand. This time all three of us made a sweep through a different area of wood — again without success.

At the end of each draw we discussed possibilities. By then we knew for certain that the calf had not had any sustenance since it parted from its mother eighteen hours earlier. How much longer could it hold out? The farmer thought it might have a better chance if it had never sucked at all — if it was still existing on its inborn reserves, and its digestive system had not yet been activated by a dose of milk. He recalled how, in a similar incident twenty years ago, a calf which had never fed had survived four days before being found.

Not until you start searching an area of hill country for one small refugee do you realise how daunting the task is. A hundred policemen, advancing shoulder to shoulder as at the scene of a crime, might well have found the calf quickly, but even they would have had a struggle in the woods on our roof-like slopes.

With only two or three people, the job seemed endless. A single bramble bush or clump of stinging nettles would hide the calf: any small depression or ditch or fragment of old wall could conceal it. Every potential hiding place had to be investigated, and the possibilities were infinite.

As a new-born heifer, the animal was worth only about £100. Yet its financial value was hardly the point. What tore at everyone's heart was the fact that its life had scarcely begun, and that, through no fault of its own, it was threatened in infancy with a miserable, lingering death.

Night fell with the position unchanged. Blanks had been drawn in all the woods, all the fields, along all the likely hedges. In desperation the farmer drove out to the small clump of trees, some distance away, in which the fugitive of twenty years earlier had eventually been discovered — without success.

During the night the weather broke. Until then the days had been warm and still. Now heavy rain set in, and hopes of finding the calf alive fell even lower. By morning, forty-eight hours had passed since its birth, thirty-six since it could have had any nourishment. Would not the cold downpour finish it off?

Unable to give up hope, I took the dogs out after breakfast on a wider-than-usual trajectory which brought us up a different, wooded ravine leading towards the point of disappearance. Mist hung heavily on the escarpment, and in the murk under the dripping trees every log looked like a brown body.

Again, I felt that we had to try every small patch of ground cover, for whereas a wounded wild animal like a deer will get up and run if something approaches it closely, I felt sure that the calf must by then be so weak that it would not move at all. At the top of the hill I met the farmer's son, coming across the field for the umpteenth time.

Then, just as hope was dying, the miracle occurred. At midday, of its own accord, the calf suddenly came out from where it had been lying all the time, not fifty yards from the farm buildings, tucked under what the farmer called the 'beddywine', or clematis, in the bottom of the hedge, half way up the side of the triangular field. Far from taking off into the hinterland, it had never gone anywhere. Searchers had passed its lair innumerable times.

Reunited with its mother, it began to suck as though nothing had happened, and she accepted it as though it had never left her side. The cost of the search — in man-hours and nervous energy — was better not calculated, but the relief in which it ended was inexpressible.

Two Wheels Best

Our rendezvous was hardly inspiring: outside the gates of the Anchor Butter headquarters on an industrial estate in the fringes of Swindon — a soulless place of wide, anonymous roads and cavernous buildings without faces. Yet within a couple of minutes my two guides had spirited me into another world, largely of their own creation.

They were Anne Billingham, leading light of the Swindon Bicycle Group, and Philip Insall, an executive of Sustrans (short for Sustrainable Transport), the charitable ginger-group in Bristol which promotes 'any action for reducing the energy consumption of transport'.

In perfect silence our cycles rolled eastwards along the disued railway line which circles Swindon's southern boundary. Immediately to our left — but mercifully out of sight and out of mind — lay the town, with its maze of roundabouts and ring-roads and fearful rush-hour traffic; to our right, grassland fell away gracefully, and beyond it in the distance loomed the Wiltshire Downs. A few other cyclists and pedestrians were on the move, but our progress could not have been easier or more peaceful.

Although Anne was too modest to make any such claim, I knew it was largely her own initiative and determination which brought this path into being. But for the lead taken by her group in 1980, part of the route would have been sold for development, and the old railway line would have been severed for ever.

As it was, the volunteers wrested permission from the Wiltshire County Council, brought in Sustrans to give expert advice, raised £4,500 from local sources, and got down to work with their own hands, clearing the track of undergrowth, restoring drains, and laying a surface of rolled limestone dust over the old shingle. Work was completed in May, 1983, but — so slow was the Council to recognise the achievement — the path was not officially adopted as a public bridleway until last year.

After a gentle ride of two-and-a-half miles in an earlier era, we suddenly re-entered the modern world in the form of another industrial estate. Anne brought out a photograph which showed that the ground on which we stood had once been Swindon Old Town Station: there in her picture, taken in the

1950s, was a pre-Beeching steam engine, still operating on the Midland and Southwest Junction line which carried trains in dark-red livery between Cheltenham and the South Coast.

After pausing to savour that melancholy bit of history, we set off on our main journey along the cycle route to Marlborough — a ten-mile stretch, of which about eight miles follow the old railway. This track — also the creation of Sustrans — was built largely with volunteer labour, and at minimum expense; even so, it cost £32,000 — an amount which (Philip pointed out with some chagrin) would almost pay for a two-yard stretch of the proposed widening of the M25 to four lanes.

As we pedalled between tall double hedges, sometimes in cuttings, sometimes on embankments which gave fine views, he had plenty of time to expound on the evils of transport policy in contemporary Britain. 'The trouble is, official culture in this country doesn't recognise that anything other than a car is a form of transport.

'More than half the road journeys made in Britain are under two miles long . . . All the policy-makers in Whitehall drive everywhere, or have someone to drive them . . . Our cities are grinding to a halt because no one will recognise the obvious truth that there isn't room for *everyone* to use a car . . .'

In short, Philip was lamenting the fact that there has been, so far, no official recognition of the value of the bicycle as a pollution-free means of travel, no Government directive encouraging the construction of specialised cycle networks. To someone riding agreeably towards Marlborough on a sunny morning, *not* along the horrible A345, the logic of his advocacy seemed irresistible.

Several facts about attitudes to cyclists were demonstrated by our particular route. One was that most people oppose *any* innovation, purely on principle. When the cycle group applied for planning permission to use the railway, the Parish Council of Ogbourne St George (through which we passed) put in an official objection; then, last year, the villagers gave Sustrans a donation, so thrilled were they with the success of the path. Similarly, residents on the outskirts of Marlborough first formed an action group against the project, then became ardent supporters.

Another tendency is for people to rip out the control barriers of wood and metal designed to prevent vehicles coming on to the paths at access-points. Even when quick-setting concrete is used, vandals tear up the defences before they are even completed: gypsies are particularly tiresome in this respect — although why, nobody is quite sure. It is as if they think their right of free movement along the highways is somehow being threatened. Gates are stolen with tedious and expensive regularity, but this is because of their value.

Selfish horse-riders are another menace. Wherever there is space, Sustrans provides a turf-covered bridleway alongside the cycle path; but often horses have to use the track itself, and if riders insist on going along a new section before the rolled limestone dust has had time to consolidate, their horses' hooves chop the surface into a consistency most uncomfortable for anyone on wheels.

In spite of all these hazards, the cyclists feel that they are gaining ground, and that councils all over the country are waking up to the fact that motorists cannot have everything their way indefinitely. In Sussex, for instance, Sustrans recently planned a cycle route — their first in that part of the country — at the invitation of a council. Within six months six more neighbouring councils had come to them with similar inquiries.

Not long ago there was a chief highway engineer in Swindon who used to ride to work, but was told that he should cease to do so because a bicycle did not fit his job or the image he ought to be projecting. That sort of attitude is dead now, killed by ever-increasing frustration and pollution caused by excessive numbers of cars.

By herculean efforts, Sustrans has built more than 200 miles of cycle tracks in various parts of Britain, mainly along disused railway lines; but this, Philip acknowledges, is a 'frankly pathetic amount compared with what's needed'. The irony is that only a slight shift in Government policy could bring about major changes.

At the moment, any public money allocated to cycling comes out of recreational budgets. If a fraction of transport or highway budgets were redirected, wonders could be done. For instance, one per cent of the cost of widening the M25 (£27 million, out of £2.7 billion) would create an entire national network of cycle tracks, comparable with the motorway system . . .

We were still discussing such possibilities when, after a particularly attractive stretch along a viaduct lined with trees, we suddenly arrived in Marlborough, as it were by the back door, and sat down to a hearty lunch in a pub. By then I needed no more persuading that on a fine autumn day especially, but on countless other occasions as well, two wheels are better than four.

Norfolk Beefings

We did our best for Apple Day recently, and we are still pressing every variety we can lay hands on for juice: a brew of Bramleys laced with a few Yarlington Mill cider apples (still far from ripe) is enough to put your hair on end. At this time of year there are apples everywhere — on the trees in the orchard, on the ground, on the compost heap, along the hedges and in the edges of the woods.

Yet, even in this glut, the sight of a few dark-red beauties on trees in the outskirts of Gloucester suddenly gave me pause. It was partly that I had not expected to see the remnants of an orchard flourishing in that dreary industrial wasteland: to someone stuck in a traffic jam, it was an agreeable surprise. But even as I stared at the fruit, I realised that some deeper force was at work.

Just as smells can be powerfully evocative, and take one back unerringly to scenes and places long forgotten, so the wine-dark red of those apples was lifting me back across the years. Suddenly I was no longer in Gloucester, but on the cricket pitch which my father used to mow in the meadow outside the garden of our home in the Chilterns.

It was not the most perfect of strips — barely twenty yards long, on a slight slope, and in no way improved by the occasional passage of cattle across it or by the nocturnal excavations of rabbits. General topographical considerations meant that one could bowl from the lower end only, and a good hit from the upper end would finish up in the wood, somehow finding its way between the laths of the old sheep fence and going to ground in the brambles.

Yet to me, aged eight or nine, that pitch might have been Lords or the Oval, so much was it the centre of my cricketing world. We mowed it and rolled it reverently, and on it, with my father patiently bowling uphill, I developed a passion for the game.

Beside the bowler's run-up — where mid-on should have been — there stood an apple tree of considerable antiquity. I cannot remember it ever being whole: in my earliest recollection, half the trunk has split away, showing healed, grey wounds, and its few surviving branches all hang over on the same side. After every winter storm it became still more decrepit, until it was little more than a skeleton.

The extraordinary thing about the tree was that every year it bore fruit. Others might fail, but this old wreck never failed to bring forth large, round, dark-red apples of incredible hardness. They ripened late, long after other varieties had fallen off, but even if we left them until the end of November, they were still like bullets, perfectly inedible raw, and not much good even when cooked.

They were known locally as 'beef' apples, which always made me suppose that they must have some tremendous strength, and be very good for you. Later research suggests that they were probably Norfolk Beefings — late-ripening cookers which are predominantly red. But they were never any use to me, except that in autumn I could sometimes palm one surreptitiously and bowl it instead of the ball.

Looking back, I realise that the whole field of about two acres must once have been planted as an orchard. By the time I grew up, many of the trees had gone, and the survivors were all senior citizens, widely spaced about the grass; but apart from the Norfolk Beefing they included two other apple trees, an enormous walnut and two whiteheart cherries.

In early summer these last always caused me great anxiety. If their cherries ripened, they were luscious beyond dreams: huge, waxy yellow globes, flushed on one side with pink. Yet all too often they never reached maturity, being eaten in infancy by blackbirds, rooks and other airborne raiders. Only if we exercised ceaseless vigilance could we be sure of getting some for ourselves.

Then, one July evening, there took place an incident which haunts me to this day. The birds had been kept at bay; the cherries had ripened, and an intrepid man called Alan, who worked on the farm, disappeared up a ladder into the highest branches.

I never knew exactly what happened — whether the ladder broke or he just lost his balance. What I do remember is the thump of him hitting the ground, and the sight of him being carried off on a makeshift stretcher. Rumour came back that he had broken his back. Whether or not hearsay exaggerated the extent of his injuries, I am not sure, but somehow, from that moment, I felt that the cherries were dangerous, and although I could see masses of them hanging there, I did not want them any more . . .

Angry hoots jolted me back to the present. Once more I was in Gloucester, with impatient drivers behind me; but as I jolted forward I had time for one more quick, sideways look at the round, red apples which had transported me to another country.

★　★　★

To a casual passer-by the plume of smoke, rising white from the floor of the valley, looks rather fine against the blazing gold and russet of the woods which hang on the surrounding hillsides; but to a connoisseur of local affairs it resembles nothing so much as an exclamation-mark — a silent riposte from the heap of tree-roots and earth which is slowly burning away.

The pile has been there for many moons, ever since the farmer on whose land it lies reclaimed a silted-up mill-pond and turned it into a lake. For years he has been waiting for the roots to dry out before setting fire to them, and at least one former attempt to ignite them failed.

Then, two weeks ago, he needed to get rid of some contaminated straw, so he dumped it on the edge of the root-pile and set it alight. What he had failed to do earlier, the straw now did for him: in no time the whole heap was blazing, and, because it contained a number of old car tyres, it began giving off dense black smoke.

Luckily the wind was in an unusual quarter — the north-east — with the result that the smoke was borne harmlessly away from the village and into the uninhabited end of the valley. This, however, was not good enough for militant environmentalists, two of whom, both female, were very soon on the scene, ordering the fire extinguished.

The farmer obliged them by bulldozing earth and manure over the heap and dousing the flames — a feat which he completed just as two fire engines, summoned by some busybody, arrived from the nearby town. The incident was apparently over.

Not so: the fire was down but not out. Inside the heap, beneath a cap of earth, it must have been going fiercely, for a few days later it began to break out again. Heavy raid did nothing to douse it, and now it is still going well: large holes have been burnt in the canopy, whole poplar roots reduced to ash. The odds are that in a few more days nothing will be left.

From a distance, the mound looks like an outsized bonfire smouldering gently: only if you go close to it do you realise what tremendous heat has built up inside. Small, intimate squeaks, groans and exhalations keep emanating from its depths; the earth surface steams in various places, and every now and then a new jet breaks out of an area previously intact.

In some of these noises — as in the exclamatory column of smoke — I seem to detect an element of derision, as if the inferno was having the last laugh on the ladies who sought to kill it in infancy.

Loss of Rustic Appetite

The first person to whom I offered it was the young fellow who had helped me load bags of cement. As I prepared to drive off, I said, 'Fancy a pig's head?'

He pushed up the brim of his hat and gave me a funny look. 'Where is it?'

'Here'. I brought it up from the floor of the jeep. The polythene bag was still slightly frosted, but through it the waxy features of the left side of the face leered out warily, and the bristles seemed to curve up with a truculent air. All at once the man looked less than well. 'I don't think the missus'd like it,' he said faintly. 'Trying to get rid of it, are you?'

'No, no — it's just that we've got too many.'

I drove off. Little did the fellow know that *one* pig's head was too many for us. Still less could he suspect that the thing had been in slow orbit round our deep-freeze for more than a year; that whenever it had come to the surface, my wife had been unnerved by the sardonic curl of its lip; and that now I was under orders to get rid of it at all costs.

The easiest way would have been to conceal it in a shopping bag and dump it in the crusher at the council tip; yet that seemed a waste. It weighed several pounds, and a good deal of it was meat. Surely somebody would appreciate it?

Leaving the builders' merchants, I headed for home, but on the way pulled into a garage. Perhaps it was a mistake to take my offering into the pay-office: at any rate, its effect was the opposite of what I had hoped. 'Gawd!' cried the girl on the till. 'Get that thing out of here before I faint.'

I went, feeling like a leper and reflecting on the feeble state of gastronomy in the west of England. Have country people ceased to eat pigs' heads? Surely their forebears would never have rejected so tempting an offer? Does not Mrs Beeton give recipes for pig's cheek, pig's ears ('wash the ears well and soak for five-six hours'), and indeed for pig's head itself ('remove the hair, eyes, snout and brains . . .')?

Such musings did not solve my problem. The head still lay on the floor, now oozing slightly through its bag, where a passenger's feet would have been. Again I was approaching the tip . . . but once more some stubborn instinct sent me past. At last, though, the solution came to me: if humans spurned the last remnant of poor piggy, at least it would make a portion for foxes.

At the bottom of a hill, where a stone wall runs beside the lane, I split open the polythene wrapping, tipped the head out into the brambles, and drove away. That was a couple of days ago.

Whether or not my reject has already been eaten, I cannot say; but I would lay long odds against it surviving the weekend, as the scavengers in our woods are pretty quick off the mark. Foxes, badgers, stray dogs, rats, owls, crows, magpies . . . together, they clean up carrion at astonishing speed.

Altogether, the eating power latent in the countryside is formidable — and I never saw it more impressively displayed than in Co. Tipperary, when a donkey once died during the winter and the farmer, with typical fecklessness, left its body lying in a field.

One might have been on the plains of the Serengeti, rather than in the Emerald Isle, so fast did that carcase vanish: during the day I never saw anything feeding on it except birds, and presumed that the main demolition must had been carried out at night; but within a week it had been reduced to a skeleton, and then even the bones began to be spirited away.

I know that we have no lions or hyenas in Gloucestershire; even so, I feel confident that my pig's head will furnish one or more wild creatures with a slap-up dinner, and that not much of it will survive till Monday morning.

★ ★ ★

The most obvious advantage of having cats about the farmyard is that they terrorise rats and mice. Never mind that, when I come downstairs in the morning, the sound of chair-covers being ripped up is loud in the land, and that every flat surface is covered with muddy footprints. Outside, the little fiends certainly earn their keep.

Yet besides making a practical contribution to the economy, they also provide endless amusement. Consider Rosie — who at rest resembles a tabby powder-puff with a snowy waistcoat, mounted on very small white rollers. Curled up on a sofa, she does not look as though she could break out of an amble; but watch her race up the trunk of the yew tree, ears flat, eyes rolling, tail thrashing, and you see she has entered another world.

That is the point: by their tremendous excitement, the cats transform the farmyard. To us humans, it is a modest collection of stone buildings set round three sides of a rectangle. To them, it is an adventure playground on a huge scale, a combination of artificial assault course and natural jungle, with unlimited scope for improvisation.

Jasper, going like smoke along the tops of the walls, obviously fancies he is on a motorway. Rosie, grappling with the highest branches of the flowering cherry, is clearly possessed by atavistic excitement, imagining herself to be a tiger or a leopard. Even their mother, though relatively staid, often scoots from one building to the next as though the ground were red hot.

It is also true that Rosie has set up her outdoor headquarters in a tunnel in the hay bales, from which we cannot bear to dislodge her. This means that it is impossible to use hay from the front of the stack, and activity in that area is all-but paralysed. Yet this, we feel, is a small price to pay for the fun of having our environment so greatly expanded by feline antics and enthusiasm.

November

Roots in the Chalk

Like A.E. Housman and his land of lost content, I see it shining plain: the chalk-and-flint hill country in which I grew up. Three years have passed since we left it. I am now happily settled in another home, and have become very fond of my new surroundings; yet so indelibly is that earlier landscape printed on my memory that it floats into my mind every day, and often into dreams as well.

It is not merely the shapes of wood and field, the lie of hill and valley and lane, that return so clearly. What puts everything into still sharper focus is the endless succession of incidents with which I associate particular places. Walk down into the wood with me, and you will see what I mean.

The first plantation is Duffy's Hangar, named after me. The spruce look sickly, and the reason is not far to seek: this area was once the rick-yard of the farm, and generations of straw, rotting down, have left the ground too soggy for trees to grow well. Here, on a never-to-be-forgotten night, the ricks caught fire, and in the turmoil our cat, propelled by a mixture of fear and excitement, rushed so high up an ancient pear tree that only the firemen could get it down . . .

On a few yards, and we are in a plantation of larch. A little way along the grass track is the scene of another famous incident — when Old Bert's tractor went up in flames. One hot summer's day the 'bloody old fool', as he was affectionately known, had been cutting the undergrowth between the lines of trees with a swipe, whose whirling chains rip off everything over which they pass.

According to him, he had switched off his engine and walked home to lunch — only to find, on his return, a smouldering wreck, apparently ignited by the sun shining through one of the cab's windows. Other people felt that Bert had himself set fire to the tractor accidentally, or that, when it had burst into flames spontaneously, he had bolted for home.

Either way, the big back tyres had vanished, and the intense heat generated by rubber and oil burning had melted the windscreen, leaving a pool of glass, molten and then reformed, seared into the turf. The scars endured for months afterwards . . .

On a bit more, and we are at the point where I myself, swiping the ride one autumn, nearly perished through a freak accident. A lump of wood, accelerated with immense force by the whirling chains, escaped the casing of the swipe, ricocheted vertically off the inside of one back wheel and caught me a stunning blow on the jaw.

For a few seconds the world went black; but mercifully, as I swayed forward in my seat, I automatically stamped my left foot on the clutch and brought the tractor to a halt. Had I been knocked out cold, the possible consequences scarcely bear thinking about: if I had tumbled forward, the tractor and swipe might have gone crawling over me . . .

Now, only quarter of a mile out, we have reached the boundary of the larch plantation. Once, when an earlier generation of beech trees still stood, a squirrel shoot took place here. A boy of eleven, I was proudly carrying a single-barrel 28-bore, a handy but lightweight weapon. When a squirrel was sighted at the very top of one of the trees, the gamekeeper thrust his own gun — an old, double-barrelled 12-bore with Damascus barrels — into my hands and said, 'Go on, Duffy. Give 'im one with that!'

When I raised the huge gun to my shoulder and fired, the recoil sent me reeling: head spun, eyes smarted, collar-bone ached. But everyone said, 'Well done!' and through my tears I felt I had suddenly become a man . . .

Hurry, now, for time and space are running out. Down this path is the single holly bush from which a grand fallow buck burst out one winter morning as I walked past. Snow exploded from the dark-green leaves as he broke cover, and his feet crunched magnificently into the frozen leaves as he went bounding away . . .

Here, beside the bottom ride, where in spring bluebells flood the valley like an inland sea, a pile of cordwood once came alive with stoats. We watched in amazement as five, six, seven of the little creatures, lithe and fast as gingery snakes, went whipping round and round the logs — a whole family at play . . .

Here, where the wood narrows to a point, the forces of law and order once stood baffled, having driven the covert for fox, which had been seen going in there. As the keepers and farm-hands gathered round one last small patch of brambles, loudly declaring that they were buggered if they knew how the blighter had escaped them, the briars at their feet began to heave, and out went Reynard, slipping away up a hedge on such a crafty line that no one could get a shot at him . . .

We have not even left the first wood, one of dozens. We have not entered any of the fields, all of whose names I know. We are still a long way from the spot at which the estate's first Land-Rover — then regarded as a new-fangled miracle, and unstoppable — sank to its roof in an old dew-pond camouflaged by leaves; and still farther from the glade among rhododendrons where, one winter, we flushed out a Polish prisoner-of-war who had become so eccentric as to foresake his hutted camp and live in the woods like an animal, sleeping in a roll of hay . . .

This is the whole trouble: a hundred other incidents crowd in upon me, and I know they always will; for those blue remembered hills are not only imprinted on my memory: their every contour is graven on my heart.

Defending your Acres

From every quarter of the compass come cries of despair, uttered by people who have been steam-rollered in their attempts to keep patches of the countryside intact. Given the complexity of planning laws, and the number of bodies devoted to conservation, it seems extraordinary that private citizens are still so helpless when it comes to defending their territory.

Witness the bitter experience of the Cotswold Water Park Villages' Society, formed three years ago to fight the threat of a £100 million development in the area of farmland and lakes south of Cirencester. The proposal put up by Lakewoods was (and is) for a holiday village of 600 chalets, with beds for 3,500 people, a seventy-bedroom hotel and a central facility housing (among other things) a swimming-pool and eight restaurants.

So great was local alarm over this idea that the new society rapidly recruited 1,200 members and raised a total of £33,000 in its attempt to ward off the monster. In a sparsely-populated rural area, the collection of such funds was no mean feat.

And what did it achieve? Nothing. The villagers were chargrined to find that at the public inquiry held earlier this year their expensively-prepared evidence was entirely disregarded. The inspector seemed to pay no attention to their arguments, and on 15 August the Secretary of State for the Environment,

Michael Heseltine, granted outline planning permission for the scheme to go ahead.

All that money and effort had gone up in smoke. Now the best that the villagers can hope for is that Lakewoods will proceed first with a similar development planned for Yorkshire, and that hellfire may somehow strike the company before it gets round to wrecking the water park. There is not room here even to list the arguments advanced by either side at the inquiry: all that can be said for certain is that commercial rapacity has triumphed over concern for the environment.

The same looks set to happen in and around Market Drayton. There the North Shropshire District Council has scented what it describes as 'a golden opportunity' for putting its fortunes in order. Its aim is to sell the historic Smithfield, or cattle-market, in the centre of the town to a development company, who will replace it with — guess what — a 28,000 square foot supermarket, a car park and some low-cost housing. In return, the developers will build a new cattle market, lorry park and swimming pool off the A53 on the town's southern outskirts.

Whether or not the changes will destroy the character of the town-centre is a matter for local debate — and there will be vociferous opposition when the Council holds a public meeting to discuss the issue on Monday. The Wednesday market has been the focus of social and commercial life in Market Drayton since time immemorial. But of far wider concern to conservationists is the fact that the out-of-town installations are to be built on part of Fordhall Farm, the property managed for fifty years by that veteran agricultural innovator Arthur Hollins.

Arthur has developed a unique system of grassland management. This uses no chemicals – see page 62 – and, far from impoverishing the soil, gradually builds up its fertility by natural means. In other words, over the years he has developed a cheap, effective and environmentally-sound form of good husbandry, which has attracted worldwide interest.

Arthur, unfortunately, does not own the farm: he and his family have been tenants of Fordhall for generations. Now his landlord is prepared to sell some of his ground — a move which, for the working farmer, will amount to compulsory purchase.

Arthur himself, now seventy-six, is doing what he can to forestall disaster. Meanwhile his fans, who are legion, angrily point out that there are any number of less interesting and valuable farms in the area on which the new cattle market could be dumped, and insist that commercial considerations should not be allowed to obliterate something of long-lasting environmental value.

A third *cri de coeur* comes from Cheshire, where villagers have been driven to their wits' end by motor-cycle scrambling. According to a correspondent, the trouble began in August, when she noticed strange men setting out sticks in the sloping field which faces her kitchen window.

It turned out that the farmer had given a scrambling club permission to use the field as a race-track. From the bikers' point of view, the site was as good as any other; from that of the people living in the village, it could not have been worse.

For one thing, the field — a steep, uncultivated bank dotted with interesting flowers — lay in the middle of a conservation area. For another, it had a badger sett right in the centre. A third disadvantage was that it formed part of a natural amphitheatre, so that noise was bound to be maximised.

The villagers supposed that because all building was under such tight control, there must be some planning law which they could invoke to stop the races. As my correspondent puts it, people building extensions to their houses 'have to match brick for brick, slate for slate', and the local pub had been required to remove an artificial tree put up to amuse children.

Yet every attempt to prevent mass invasion by bikers proved useless. Inquiries revealed that up to fourteen meetings a year could be run without any consent. The village united in protest. The farmer refused to discuss the matter with the Parish Council. The District Council sent out tree-preservation officers, countryside preservation officers, highway inspectors. The Noise Abatement Society gave legal advice . . . all in vain.

The meeting was held on a Sunday. From 9 am to 5 pm unsilenced 500 cc machines tore up and down the steep banks, thirty-six at a time, in races lasting fifteen minutes. As a concession to the Church, they did lay off during the hour of the service, but at all other times the noise was beyond belief. Even indoors, conversation was impossible.

Then something happened which nobody had foreseen. The bikes tore through the thin soil on the bank and churned into the red sand beneath. After the fine weather, the sand was very dry and took to the air in the form of dust. Red clouds began to fill the valley, coating houses and cars with fine powder, which also crept in through doors and windows. By evening the whole village had turned red.

The event left locals stunned and incredulous. How could such violence be inflicted on them? To their infinite relief, the Environmental Health Officer later decided that, under the terms of the 1990 Environmental Protection Act the pall of dust and the outrageous increase in noise (to between 2,000 and 3,000 times the normal level) both constituted 'statutory nuisances', and announced that the District Council would take out an abatement order to prevent further meetings being held.

One small victory for country people, then — but a dearly-bought one. Meanwhile, in a thousand other places scattered through Britain, battles like those of Fordhall Farm and the Cotswold Water Park are being fought through; and it is a sad but safe bet that in most of them that least attractive of human failings — greed — will be the victor.

Arcadian Brew

The place calls to mind the single hexameter line by Horace which became a Roman proverb: *Non cuivis homini contingit adire Corinthum.* Not just anyone, wrote the old poet, was lucky enough to visit the Greek city of Corinth, then one of the world's wonders.

With his love of simple country things, he might have said the same of the Donnington Brewery, nestling in a fold of the hills near Stow-on-the-Wold, in Gloucestershire: few people have the good fortune to go there, for it is a private concern, and its proprietor, Claude Arkell, is a very private person.

A tall, upright, grey-haired man, of distinguished appearance and quietly spoken, now in his seventies, he looks more like a don or scientist than brewer. Apart from anything else, he seems far too slender to have built his career around ale. Yet a few minutes' conversation show that here is a man absolutely in tune with his calling, and with the lovely surroundings in which he works and lives.

Imagine a shallow, curving valley dammed at its lower end to produce a four-acre mill-pond. The water, all from springs, is crystal-clear. Swans sail over its surface, some black, some white. Monstrous trout, up to 8lb in weight, cruise like sharks in its pellucid depths.

Beside the dam stands the brewery, once a wool mill, then a corn mill, made of honey-coloured stone.

Almost everything about the place is agreeably old-fashioned: nothing so modern as a typewriter disfigures the office, where correspondence is done by hand.

What is more, water-power from the mill wheels is still used to drive pumps and work the hoists which raise malt to the mash-tun.

To stand in the heart of the old mill, below water level, is to travel effortlessly into the past. Outside , the sluice of the race is closed, but still a trickle of water finds its way into the buckets of the wheel on the outer wall, so that every now and then it gives a turn. Suddenly, the 8ft wheel inside the wall also begins to revolve, its greased, applewood cogs noiselessly engaging the worm-gear that takes off the drive.

Brewing began here in 1865, when one branch of the Arkell family moved up from Wiltshire, where they were already established as brewers near Swindon. Richard Arkell, who came north to Donnington, was only one of the pioneers in that generation: others set up breweries in Canada and Australia.

The enterprise at Donnington flourished, and Claude Arkell is the grandson of Richard. As he remarks, beermaking in the old days was rooted in the local community. Not only were the brewers themselves farmers: they got most of their business from other farmers and from the big houses round about.

In Wiltshire Honest John Arkell was said to have acquired many of his pubs through hunting accidents: every time he fell off his horse ('bought a piece of ground', in hunting vernacular) and was taken to a hostelry to recover, he ended up buying the inn.

In Gloucestershire Richard also did much business in the hunting-field, keeping a note-book in his pocket and taking orders for beer as the field waited beside a covert.

The trouble was, the farmers would never part with money. Rather than pay up, they would wait till the next harvest, then parade at the brewery with a nice sample of malting barley, hoping to settle their debts by supplying a ton or two of grain. By this means, they guaranteed themselves twelve months' credit.

The other main customers were the landed squires. 'Business was all with the hierarchy in the mansions round about,' Claude recalls. 'Big houses were full of slaves, then. Servants didn't get paid much, but they did get bags of beer. The owners would buy it in thirty-sixes (36-gallon barrels) — bloody great things. The idea was to get the servants half-cut so that they didn't mind so much about money and forgot the score.'

When Claude's father died in 1952, the business was hit hard. Apart from the brewery, the old man had owned 500 acres of land and several houses. His estate was valued at £82,000, and duty payable set at £45,000. Claude was forced to sell 170 acres, three cottages and some Dutch barns, all for £11,000, and to take out a long-term agricultural mortgage.

Since then, as he puts its, he has 'staggered on' — and pretty well, too. He still has the brewery, 300 acres, and fifteen pubs in the villages and towns round about.

On paper he is a millionaire, but claims to have no money, saying it 'goes out as fast as it comes in'. Not that this seems to worry him much: he is first and foremost a brewer. Making beer, he says, is like cooking; one never ceases to learn.

After public school and a course at the Royal Agricultural College, Cirencester, he was taught the trade by his father. 'Perhaps I should have gone away to another brewery,' he reflects. 'But somehow that didn't happen.'

In the Second World War he joined the RAF and trained fighter pilots in America. Since then Donnington has been his home (he lives in a house on the edge of the mill-pond, a few yards from the brewery door.) He is married, but has no children.

His two draught bitters — BB and SBA — have remained remarkably constant over the years. Neither is particularly strong, but both have the nutty, hoppy taste that mass-produced beers cannot match. Curiously, the weaker of the two, BB, is easily the more popular. He also sells mild whenever demand warrants it.

After a lifetime in the trade, he remains fascinated by the intricacies of his profession. On the day I visited Donnington he was experimenting to see if an industrial vacuum cleaner would suck off the surplus yeast which froths up on top of the fermentation vats: to his delight, the expensive new toy was doing an excellent job.

Apart from work, his great passion is the collection of ornamental waterfowl, pheasants, peacocks and other exotic birds which live round the brewery. As he moves among them, he addresses each one, particularly delighted with the Cereopsis geese, which emit extraordinary grunts, like pigs.

He is renowned as a fisherman — and indeed his nephew, Jim Arkell, now managing director of the Wiltshire firm, caught his first trout while training for a year at Donnington. Claude, he remembers, had a magical touch at tickling trout — the art of reaching down stealthily into the stream and catching the fish by suddenly closing a hand around the body.

In Claude's reckoning, a 4lb wild fish, smoked, is the most delicious thing you can eat, and far superior to salmon.

He admits to drinking a pint and a half of his own brews every day, but agrees that he, being a beanpole, is a poor advertisement for them.

To a visitor, he seems the perfect advertisement for a way of life that many people would love to emulate but almost none will know: an existence of skilled and steady effort in surroundings of rare beauty.

My own memories of Donnington are not just of the mellow stone buildings and the intoxicating smell of hops that permeates them. Rather, I think of the place's Arcadian peace — of mill-wheels turning in a gentle rush of water, of swans calling over the glassy pond, and of deep-bellied trout cruising beneath them in water clear as gin.

Feuds over Pheasants

It is a curious fact that although hunting people often become involved in unseemly public rows, such as the one which has recently rocked the Quorn, shooting men are rarely seen to engage in internecine skirmishes. Considering that far more people shoot than hunt, and that bitter feuds smoulder for years between rival estates or syndicates, it seems all the more odd that so few disputes are reported.

There are, I suppose, two main reasons. First, shooting is a less contentious sport than hunting, so that it naturally attracts less attention; and second, conflicts tend to be small-scale affairs between neighbours, which grind on and on without outsiders becoming aware of them.

The point was brought home to me when we moved house six winters ago. Scarcely had we arrived than there appeared a young fellow clad in a kammo jacket who announced himself to be a member of a local syndicate. Was I a shooting man, he asked?

I assured him that I was, and that for the past dozen years I had run a shoot in another part of the country. 'Good!' he exclaimed. 'Then you'll understand what I'm saying.'

His message was that he and his colleagues had the rights in part of the valley, where they operated with the utmost decorum. The rest of the ground, however, was rented by a rival syndicate, and he wished me to understand that a more villainous mob of trespassers and poachers had never existed, in Gloucestershire or anywhere else. In their efforts to lure birds over the boundary, he told me, there was no low trick to which these cowboys would not descend.

I murmured that I had come across such people before, and would look out for them — whereupon he added, 'Oh, by the way, will it be all right if we stand a gun in your top field when we do the wood on the hill?'

I said this would be fine, and off he went. But within half an hour I was confronted by another kammo-clad stranger, who announced himself to be a member of the opposition. He, too, asked if he might station a gun in my top field when his lot were doing *their* part of the wood; and, with permission secured, he launched into a diatribe against the people across the lane.

Even if I thought I had met some crooks in my time (he warned me), I had never seen scheisters half as despicable as these. Villains to a man, as unscrupulous as they were unspeakable, they would practically steal the wheels off my car while I was sitting in it.

I did not let on that he was repeating practically verbatim the slanders uttered by his predecessor half an hour earlier. Nor did I inquire about the alleged misdemeanours of the opposition, as I knew from experience what these must be.

The fact is that if one rears pheasants with considerable labour and expense, and does one's best to keep the birds at home, it is extremely annoying to lose them: bad enough to find that they are wandering away of their own accord, but an appalling provocation to see them being lured by foul means.

These include the placing of feed-hoppers at strategic points close to the boundary, and, in extreme cases, the laying of trails of corn across the frontier (wheat laced with aniseed is deadly). A legitimate but underhand trick is to plant patches of cover such as kale just the right distance — maybe 100 yards — from someone else's wood: the birds will naturally move out to the crop to feed, and can be cut off as they head for home.

This sort of thing has been going on steadily all round us for the past six years, with occasional outbursts when irritation becomes too great to be contained. In one incident Team A planted a patch of kale across a right-of-way occasionally used by Team B, and fenced the patch in with wire to keep cattle out — only to find that the wire soon finished in a tangled mass at the bottom of the hill.

On another occasion the ringleader of one team was spotted deep in enemy territory, driving birds back to base with his dog at first light. Elaborate plans were laid to trap him, should he try the manoeuvre again; but he, perhaps realising that he had been rumbled, was either too wise or too windy to repeat the performance.

To uncommitted outsiders, all this must sound extraordinarily childish — as indeed it is; and the sad truth about the feud in question is that both shoots would be immeasurably improved if they joined forces, so that instead of squabbling over the terrain, they could use it properly.

This they will never do, at least while the present incumbents remain in charge. Ill-feeling between the factions runs too deep — and I know that it is reflected in hundreds of similar confrontations up and down the country.

Mutual jealousy and suspicion may die down when the pheasant season ends next week, but, sure as fate, they will blaze up again come autumn.

★   ★   ★

Who should turn up the other morning but a previous owner of our house. Gone these twenty years to Australia, he reappeared on holiday with his wife, son and daughter-in-law, and asked — with many apologies for disturbing us — if he might look round.

He need not have apologised. His visit was a delight, for it led to numerous revelations about the house, the outbuildings and the land.

The son, now thirty-one, suffered that experience familiar to all grown-ups who return to childhood haunts, of finding that the whole place had shrunk. His wife — an attractive Australian girl — seemed delighted with the antiquity of the house. But the two parents went about wide-eyed with memory, each visibly struggling to reconcile individual recollections with what they could see.

The outside of the house remains much as it was when they had it; but another family who lived here after them and before us changed the inside a good deal. Where, our visitors asked, had the back staircase gone? We were none too sure. And what had happened to the steps which went down to the cellar outside the sitting room? This was more easily explained, for the room had been extended by the removal of an internal wall, and access to the cellar is now through a trap-door.

The mystery of the kitchen floor was soon solved. I have often wondered why the flagstoned floor falls so steeply from one corner to the other, and now I learnt that the slope was for drainage: once the farm dairy, the room used to be part of what is now our dining-room, next door, and the whole floor used to be sloshed-down to a drain in the corner.

A walk round the yard sparked many reminiscences. We did not like to bring up the fact that it was bovine tuberculosis, apparently passed to the milking cows by badgers, which had forced our visitor to give up his dairy farm and move to Australia. There was enough to talk about without that.

But what stopped him in his tracks was the sight of the old red tractor, a Massey-Ferguson 65. Once his, now mine, it was still in business, aged at least thirty. The man was flabbergasted, especially when I turned the starter-key and the engine burst into life.

At that cheerful roar, the years fell away: for a few moments he seemed uncertain which end of the earth he was at. As he left, he was kind enough to say that we had made his morning — but I did not exaggerate in the least when I replied that he had made ours.

Too Many Walkers

Whenever the weekend weather is fine, the wily woodland deerstalker stays at home: he may get away with a successful foray at dawn on Saturday, but thereafter the woods are liable to become so infested by walkers and joggers, riders and cyclists that armed expeditions are both potentially dangerous and a waste of time.

Knowing this, I still went out last Saturday in the hope that I might defeat the odds and make some progress with my cull of fallow does, with which I am behind schedule. The afternoon was glorious: air crisp, sun bright, and the ground soft underfoot after recent rain.

As I drove down into the steep valley, my heart sank, for, as I had feared, there were people coming and going in all directions: a girl being half run-away-with on a white horse, a hiker in red stockings, an elderly couple who had parked in a glade and were pottering with a poodle. Most of the wanderers were on legitimate footpaths or bridleways, and it was pointless to remonstrate with those who were mildly trespassing: the only sensible course was to slip away to an area which seemed less likely to have been disturbed.

I had been creeping cautiously downhill for only about five minutes when I became aware of deer above me. I say 'became aware', because that is what happens if one advances at the traditional stalker's pace of two steps backward for every one forward: one does not *see* the deer so much as realise that they are in view.

Scanning with binoculars, I became aware that the head of a fallow doe was visible about ninety yards above me. The animal's body was hidden by undergrowth, but I could also make out a couple of backsides, given away by the tell-tale black-and-white striped pattern of tails and hind-quarters.

It looked as if the small herd included some half-dozen animals, and at least one shootable doe. The deer were in range, but they were on the skyline and in a position far too dangerous for a shot: even a perfectly-placed rifle bullet would probably go straight through its target and on over the open country above.

What to do, then? The doe had seen my head, and was watching intently. At least, she had seen a movement, which had roused her suspicions. I hoped that if I kept still for a minute or two she would assume that what she had spotted was an innocuous hiker who had gone on out of sight.

If she did come to this conclusion, the odds were that she would remain where she was, giving me a chance to duck down and manoeuvre — for I have often noticed that deer are not alarmed by the passage of people whom they consider harmless, or by routine operations such as those of gamekeepers feeding pheasants. If someone walks straight through a wood without stopping, deer will stand and watch — but they have an extraordinary knack of distinguishing surreptitious or evasive movements from innocent ones, and will take off the moment they sense danger.

I stood still and waited. Zephyr the labrador, sitting by my feet, was well out of the deer's sight. From high in the distance a buzzard whistled, and pigeons came gliding over the trees on their way to roost.

Then suddenly a movement caught my eye. On the skyline to my right something had passed between two trees — yet another illustration of how movement attracts attention, and of how much better it is for a stalker to remain still for as long as he can.

My glasses revealed a solitary hiker in navy-blue donkey jacket swinging northwards along a footpath above the old-horse-paddock which nestles on a slope surrounded by trees. It was clear from his manner that he had not seen the deer, but he was going to pass so close to them that, harmless as he was, he would be bound to shift them.

Quickly I realised that his arrival might rebound to my advantage: as he passed above the deer, he might push them down the hill towards me. It so happened that I was within a few yards of a high seat — a ladder with a small platform on top, propped against a larch tree — and I resolved that the moment the deer began to run, I would nip up the ladder to a better vantage-point.

A loud, gruff alarm-bark ricocheted through the wood. There was a flurry of movement as the deer started to mill about. In ten seconds I was up the high seat, rifle at the ready . . .   but no: like an ill-struck billiard ball, he had put pressure on the herd at slightly the wrong angle and bounced them along the slope to the north instead of downwards.

Still, I knew roughly where they would have gone, and after a ten-minute wait for them to settle, I set off in pursuit. Presently I again saw a tell-tale backside protruding over a ridge. This one, though, had antlers above it: a good buck which I did not want to shoot. But a few minutes' observation revealed that he was with some does, and that this was the same little herd.

Once more I was pinned down, unable to advance until the group moved over the crest. By then the sun was nearly on the horizon behind me, and the western sky was flaring up in a blaze of orange. Deep in the wood shadows were flooding into hollows and thickening among the tree-trunks.

Just as I hoped that all other humans had gone home, up from the valley piped the voice of a child, poisonously querulous and loud. The buck heard it, of course, and turned his head to glare down at the source, which soon revealed itself as a couple muffled to the eyeballs and beyond in hooded anoraks, dragging a recalcitrant junior pedestrian between them.

Their progress was agonisingly slow. Hard as I might will them to hurry up and disappear before the light had gone, they moved like snails along the lower path, stopping frequently to expostulate with the child, which from its size looked to be only five or six years old.

I took care that they did not see me or my dog, and naturally they did not spot the deer; but for at least ten minutes the buck watched them, and I watched the buck. As the sun set, a tremendous crimson glow in the western sky turned the fur on his neck from white to pink and blazed off his dark eyes. In all that time he never moved, except to twitch an ear. Confident as he was that the bawling nipper posed no threat to him, he yet wished to see it off his patch before relaxing.

Frost began to bite. Pheasants were going up to roost all round us, the cocks ratcheting out their staccato calls. From somewhere on top of the wood came the dry *roff, roff, roff* of a dog fox setting out on his night-round in search of a mate.

Already it was too late to shoot, almost too late to see; but through the binoculars I caught a flurry of movement as the buck turned, his antlers black now among the black branches and stems. One stick cracked as he shifted, and then he was gone, no doubt on his way up to the grass field in which he had been grazing at night.

By the time I reached my vehicle, full dark had fallen; but even though I had got nothing, I felt that my time had been far from wasted. To have been out on that glorious afternoon, to have observed the deer adroitly dealing with the weekend invasion of their territory by humans, to have blended for a couple of hours into the life and fabric of the wood — all that had made the excursion a hundred times worthwhile.

December

Alas, Poor Shalimar

He ate his own weight in peanuts many times over. He stripped every wallflower in the garden to its stalk. He attacked any new car which ventured into the yard, and, if not repelled, inflicted fearful damage on its paintwork. In the spring he made the most appalling noise for weeks on end, and whenever he managed to father any chicks, he did his best to kill them. His habits, in a phrase, were by no means endearing — and yet we loved him.

Shalimar the peacock's appearance was so splendid that walkers would stop and gawp when they saw him lording it on the terrace, and motorists sat transfixed as they found an immense bird parading ahead of them up the lane. Now he is dead, and much lamented; but we take comfort from the fact that we helped him enjoy a good life.

He came to us, along with two females, as part of the fallout from a study done by a department of Oxford University in the park at Nuneham Courtenay. What the researchers made of him, I do not know, but if they had continued their observations through the years, they would have discerned a fairly curious character.

We then lived in a farmhouse surrounded by woods and fields, with no human neighbours at all — an ideal environment for peacocks. Our new recruits soon mastered the first essential of survival — the habit of roosting high in trees, without which they would soon have been eaten by foxes — but it was not long before Shalimar began to display unpleasant signs of aggression, particularly whenever one of the chickens brought off a brood of young, which he would do his best to murder.

It was this habit which almost led to his premature demise. One May my wife went off for a short holiday, leaving me in charge. Hardly had she disappeared when I found Shalimar attacking some baby chicks. To scare him off, I picked up a light stick about fifteen inches long and flicked it at him backhand.

Had I practised the throw a thousand times, I could never have repeated what I achieved by accident. As the stick flew towards the peacock, it rotated slowly, and one end caught him smack on the back of the head. Down he went in a heap.

'My God!' I thought. 'Now I *am* in trouble. I have killed this pampered bird within minutes of his mistress leaving him.'

Rushing forward, I picked him up. His head and neck hung down limply, but I could feel that he was still breathing, and I just had time to reflect on the fact that one does not often hold a live peacock in one's hands when suddenly he began to revive. Struggling free of my grasp, he scrabbled and fluttered up one side of a barn roof, perched unsteadily on the ridge, fell off and rolled down the other side, only to right himself and stagger away.

Clearly he was a survivor — and so it proved. Every spring brought fresh disasters: hens snatched by foxes as they sat on their nests, peachicks killed by cats, rats or dogs. Yet always Shalimar came through, and when we moved house in the winter of 1985, he was the first bird into the horsebox, individually bagged in a hessian sack.

For the purpose of keeping king-sized, semi-wild poultry, our new home was not quite so ideal. Again, it was (and is) a farmhouse set among woods and fields, but we do have one neighbour — and even though he is an exceptionally good-natured man, relations inevitably became strained by the extravagance of the peacocks' behaviour.

Vernal screeching was bad enough, avian horticulture something else — for it is as gardeners that peacocks create most havoc. Their appetite for wallflowers is insatiable, and they have a maddening habit of nipping off bright-coloured flowers and buds but then dropping them uneaten. If three or four birds decide to have a dust-bath in the row of carrots or lettuces which you have just painstakingly sown, you can say goodbye to the crop: craters eighteen inches wide make the site look like a scale model of the battle of the Somme.

Such outrages, more or less bearable on home territory, became intolerable when repeated in our neighbour's garden, especially when Shalimar's daughter Moti reared a brood of chicks on his territory. Product of incest though they were, all three grew into strapping young cock birds.

Our neighbour remained commendably calm, but there came a point at which our own nerve cracked, and we decided we must shift the family to friends in Oxfordshire who had volunteered to take them over.

This, in due course, we managed — only to hear that the peacocks caused havoc in their new environment. Moti wandered off on her own and disappeared, presumably eaten by a fox, but her sons marched overland to the village of Church Hanborough and established themselves comfortably in the gardens there, splitting the community down the centre by their presence. While half the villagers demanded their immediate removal, the other half swore they would attack anyone who laid hands on them. In the end, with great difficulty, their new owner caught them and took them away to the Child Beale reserve near Reading.

Their departure left Shalimar on his own. For a while we were afraid that he might be lonely, but by then he was well on in years, and in any case had become a family pet. Also, he allied himself closely with the chickens, sparring with the cockerels in spring and displaying at the hens. (He would also display at chaffinches or sparrows which came to pinch his food, and which remained unruffled, in spite of the fact that they were about a twentieth of his size.)

His passion for assaulting cars lasted to the end. This tiresome habit seemed to be inspired neither by a lust for infanticide nor by a hatred of specific marques: what goaded the bird was narcissism or jealousy. Just as he would see phantom rivals reflected in the downstairs windows of the house, and go for them, battering on the glass until his beak bled, so he would dimly detect another peacock lurking in the shiny paintwork of visiting automobiles, and stab viciously at it. When my daughter and son-in-law acquired a scarlet Mazda MX-5, they had to barricade it in whenever they arrived, to save it being lacerated.

Shalimar remained militant until his last few days. Then he began to mope. He would not eat, and our efforts to dose him with antibiotics were in vain. Our perennial fear — that he would become too weak to fly up to roost — at last was realised.

We never heard the tell-tale alarm call — a volley of rapidly-delivered honks — and so never knew whether he was killed during the hours of darkness or early in the morning. But after eluding foxes for more than 4,000 nights he finally fell victim to one, and all we found to mark his passing was a drift of feathers strewn across the grass beneath the apple trees.

The valley will be quieter without him, but already we feel the lack of his familiar presence. We miss him particularly in the evenings, when he would lurk about the terrace like a dark shadow before marching up to the wood for the night, and in the mornings, when he would come swooping down from his roost on set wings in a wonderful, 200-yard glide, and arrive on the lawn with a flourish. Such style, expensive as it was to maintain, lent our modest establishment a touch of class which will not be easy to replace.

A Place in the Forest

Anyone fancy living in a remote farmhouse, 900ft up in the middle of a forest on the Welsh Marches? If so, step forward: the place is standing empty, and its owners are eager to find an occupant.

Haye Park Farm, a few miles south-west of Ludlow, was no doubt once part of the extensive agricultural land round the flanks of the hill known as High Vinnals; but now it is an island, cut off on its own in the ocean of trees that constitutes Mortimer Forest. Patches of ancient oak woodland still point to the forest's medieval connection with Ludlow Castle; these were once scattered about, but since the Forestry Commission began to plant land here in the Twenties, the area covered by trees has gradually consolidated and spread to its present 3,000 acres.

To many people, mere mention of the Forestry Commission conjures up visions of dark, massed conifers. Mortimer Forest is not like that: it does include stands of pine, spruce, fir and hemlock, but it also has beech, oak and ash, and maturity has rendered its general appearance attractively open. In the north-west, where spurs run out towards the Welsh border, farmland and forest are beautifully interwoven.

Haye Park's forty acres of grass are set high among the trees; moreover, the fields border a common of about the same size, so that the island of open ground extends in all to eighty acres. Normally, anyone whose property adjoins a common has the right to graze cattle on it; but here, since the occupant of the farm is the only human residing within miles, the rights devolve on him or her alone.

The last man to live at the farm was one of the forest workers. In fact he was born in the house, and was devoted to it, leaving and returning several times until finally his wife was unable to bear its isolation any longer.

Until about three months ago, he kept 300 sheep there; but since he took them away, the fallow have moved in, and the whole place has become a luxurious deer lawn.

Anyone hoping to grow flowers or vegetables would have to build high fences to keep the animals out of the garden: as the Commission make clear, they would not accept responsibility for deer-damage.

To me, isolation is the farm's most powerful attraction. It is magnificently set apart — no neighbours, no traffic — but not shut in, for it is built on a slope and looks down on its own park-like fields, above the tops of full-grown larches, and out over miles of open country to the Malvern Hills, whose humps lie like a dragon's back on the south-eastern horizon.

If the view from Haye Park itself is stunning, that from the top of the hill, half a mile behind the farm, is still more dramatic. The summit commands a 360-degree panorama of broken hills and swooping valleys.

From the bold spur of Clee Hill in the north east, past the Long Mynd and Wenlock Edge in the north, on westwards into the wild borderlands of Wales, this is A.E. Housman country: this is his land of lost content, and from above Haye Park you see it shining plain.

Walkers and riders love the forest, since twenty miles of paths lead in all directions; and for naturalists it is a paradise, harbouring many species of birds and mammals, most conspicuously its herd of fallow deer, now 1,000 strong. Not only are deer present in large numbers: the herd includes long-haired fallow, of a type found nowhere else in the world.

According to the foresters, the house is cunningly sited, being sheltered from the prevailing south-west wind and also below the cloud-level. Even if fog is sitting on the hill-top 300ft above, the farm is usually in the clear. I myself have seen it only in winter, but I do not doubt the locals who say that in summer, with the trees alive in the breeze, and cloud-shadows dappling the plain far below, the farm is a dream of beauty.

Having no further use for the place, the Commission is anxious to dispose of it. Ideally, they would like to let it on a long lease, although at a pinch they might sell it. Either way, they intend to retain a measure of control over any occupant, for a rotter in that prime position could do them untold damage, not least by poaching the deer. Thus any disposal will be subject to certain conditions.

So far, so good. Now for some snags. Haye Park is three-quarters of a mile uphill from the nearest main road. Most of the route is a good gravel track, maintained by the Commission for their own purposes, but the last few hundred yards are slippery grass. In winter the approach could easily become impassable. Mail and milk might be delivered to the bottom of the drive, but no closer. The nearest shops are in Ludlow, five miles away.

Although there is a telephone, and water is pumped up to a reservoir above, the farm has no electricity. Anyone living there would either have to bring in the mains — at enormous cost — or survive on a generator.

The house itself is of undistinguished appearance: not ugly, but tall and rather gaunt, and lacking in charm. Its age is hard to determine. Once the property of the Salwey family, it was clearly built in several stages. A fireback in the living room is dated 1649, but may have been imported from elsewhere. Even so, parts of the building are certainly several hundred years old.

There are two large rooms on the ground floor, and three smaller ones, including a bathroom and a kitchen. The first floor also has two large rooms and two less spacious; and, on the second floor, two small rooms are tucked in under the roof. Plumbing and heating are minimal, being confined to the ground-floor kitchen and bathroom.

Considering that nearly two years have passed since the building was last inhabited, it feels and smells surprisingly dry. What worries me is its apparent fragility. Although some parts of the outside walls are faced with rendering, their basic construction seems to be of wood-frame and rubble, plastered over: internal partitions boom hollow when struck, and a rickety door, opening off the top of the stairs, gives straight on to the open air above a 20-foot drop. I have a feeling that a surveyor would throw nine fits if asked to pronounce on the house's state of health.

In the farmyard, which rises behind, the buildings are even groggier. A tiny cottage, of rose-red brick, has last seen use as a sheep-shelter, and its little rooms are sub-divided by wooden pens. A large and potentially-handsome barn, with elaborate timber trusses, turns out to be poised on the shakiest of foundations. Various other buildings, including a couple of rusty Nissen huts, are dotted about. The whole place — not to mince words — is in a frightful mess.

And yet, and yet . . . I feel strongly drawn by Haye Park's magic. With its height, its wildness, its seclusion and its myriad trees, it is exactly the kind of place in which I should love to live. Besides, its very disorder is a challenge. What satisfaction one could get from clearing it up: bulldoze most of the out-buildings, salvage good bricks and tiles, restore the barn, lay out a garden . . . Apart from anything else, it would make a marvellous summer-house — what the Welsh call a *hafod-y-coed,* a summer-place in the forest.

A real hermit, prepared to rough it, *could* live in the house as it is. But I reckon that even to stabilise the structure would cost £20,000 — and if you tried to make it comfortable, you would go through £100,000 before you got your breath back.

The Commission's main aim is to preserve the farmstead and retain its character. Having tried in vain to create some institutional role for it — as a field-study centre, for example — they now wish to hear from any individual intrepid enough to take it on.

So where are you, Mr, Mrs, Miss or Ms Green? Serious inquirers should send proposals in writing to the Marches Forest District Manager, Tim Sawyer, at Whitcliffe, Ludlow, Shropshire SY8 2HD, and be prepared to put their money where their plans are.

This article elicited many inquiries, and as a result the house was let on a long lease.

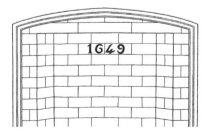

Bats in the Bomb-Bays

What have bats, bombs and precious stones in common? Normally, nothing; but in a unique development in Pembrey Forest Nature Reserve, on the shore of South Wales, bats have started to use accommodation originally designed for the storage of high explosive, under the supervision of a guardian who once prospected for diamonds.

From early in this century until the mid-fifties, a Royal Ordnance factory flourished on the flat coastal plain south-west of Llanelli, and an essential part of the establishment was a narrow-guage railway which wound in and out among the sand-dunes through a series of short, curved tunnels.

These tunnels, each about eight yards long, lined with brick and roofed with concrete slabs, were shaped to contain the blast of any accidental explosion; so strongly were they built that most remain intact forty years on. Many now lie within the boundary of the nature reserve, and last year the Forestry Commission, which owns and administers the place, had the bright idea of converting six of them into bat hibernacula.

The needs of a hibernating bat are simple: it likes a low but steady temperature, high humidity, freedom from draught and minimal disturbance. With one end walled in, and the other closed except for a small entrance slot, each tunnel is now furnished with hanging tiles and piles of broken brick, so that there are plenty of crevices into which bats can crawl.

Great was the excitement when, at the end of October, Commission staff found that their offer of free housing had been taken up: droppings, and the wings of eaten moths, showed that bats had begun to use all six tunnels, although it is still not clear whether any have actually settled in for the winter.

Anyone wanting a demonstration of how the Forestry Commission has changed its spots during the past few years should go to Pembrey and see the conservation work in progress there, for the bat experiment is only one of many projects designed to transform a purely commercial forest into a nature reserve of outstanding interest.

When the trees were planted in the 1920s and 1930s, every possible acre of sandy ground was packed with conifers, which in due course suppressed most of the natural flora of the dunes. For more than half a century everything was sacrificed to the production of timber, and only along the rides, where the sun could penetrate, did the original seed-bank remain more or less intact.

Then at last came enlightenment. In 1989 the forest was designated a nature reserve, and in 1990 a conservation ranger was appointed to take charge of it — innovations which symbolised the recent reorientation of the Commission as a whole.

The new job offered an ideal challenge to Richard Smale, a South African who before then had tried his hand at an amazing variety of occupations. Slim and dark, with neatly cropped hair and beard, he is now forty-one, but looks scarcely out of his twenties.

As a boy he was constantly exploring the bush of Northern Rhodesia, where he grew up, and he longed to be a game warden, but was advised against it by his parents, who saw no future in conservation. So he became a geological prospector, looking for copper and zinc in the wilds of Namibia.

Back in South Africa, he worked for eighteen months on an offshore oil-rig as radio-operator and medical orderly — a role for which two first-aid courses were deemed to have been sufficient training. His expertise was severely tested when a man accidentally amputated some toes: with one hand he had to tidy the patient up and keep him calm, while with the other he radioed for a helicopter.

With money saved from the rig, Smale then hitch-hiked from Cape Town to London, via Malawi, Kenya, Uganda, the Sudan and Egypt. Next came a spell as a diamond prospector in the West African Republic of Guinea, where he spent two-and-a-half years in a mud hut, enjoying life in the bush but becoming disenchanted by the destructive nature of diamond mining: in the end the sight of the rain forest being bulldozed, of rivers blown up and diverted, became too much for him.

Lured to Denmark by a Danish girlfriend, he worked there as a stevedore, gardener, janitor and organiser of a group supporting indigenous peoples. Then, feeling that it was time he 'did something worthwhile', he came to England, en-rolled for a two-year course in conservation management at Farnborough College of Technology, fell in love with Wales, and landed his present job. (His Danish friend, a translator, followed, and now lives with him as his common-law wife.)

One might imagine that after such adventures he would find the shores of South Wales rather tame. Not at all: he loves his new kingdom dearly, and is as thrilled by every discovery — for instance that of the bats in the tunnels — as if he had found a rich deposit of minerals. To him, a flock of crossbills is as rewarding as a pride of lions, the proliferation of sea buckthorn — originally imported to stabilise the sand dunes — as impressive as any plant life in the Namibian desert.

Pembrey forest certainly has powerful attractions, among them the immense sweep of white, sandy beach which bounds its south-western edge. This week, vast flocks of waders swirled and dived about the shore, and inland, the 2,500 acres of trees were loaded with a mantle of silvery hoar-frost. The forest harbours many surprises, not least the shell middens — vast heaps of empty cockles — dated by archaeologists to the thirteenth century, which show where the locals did their cooking 750 years ago.

In conservation terms, Smale has the advantage of starting from scratch, and of being backed by the Commission to do more or less what he wants. When contractors thin mature stands of timber, for instance, he can get the men to create open glades and scalloped woodland edges, thus letting in light and encouraging the regeneration of broadleaved trees such as oak, beech and alder.

Ponds are his chief delight: with infectious relish he describes how he has resuscitated the Willow Pond by pulling out old tree stumps with tractor and winch, clearing out mounds of leaf-mould and keeping down colonising plants such as yellow flag and water plantain which would reduce the area to a swamp if left unchecked.

His aim in managing the pond is many-layered: to preserve an open-water habitat for invertebrates, specifically dragonflies, which furnish prey for bats, and at the same time to provide drinking water for birds, badgers and foxes. Almost as a by-product, the work has created an attractive oasis, surrounded by flora of many kinds, among the trees.

In another project, he is experimenting to see what effect various forms of cropping have on vegetation. In a series of carefully-marked plots, he has mowed with a forage harvester and blown the mowings clear, mowed with the same machine but left the mowings on, mowed by hand and raked the mowings off, mowed by hand and left them in place. As a final variant, he imported three goats and set them to eat as hard as they could.

Such dedication now extends to every sphere of activity in Pembrey. Already the forest is changing visibly, and there can by little doubt that over the next few years, in the hands of its former diamond-hunter, it will undergo a spectacular transformation.

Henry's Homecoming

When Henry the fox terrier disappeared from his country home in East Yorkshire during a Friday morning, his mistress Sal assumed that he had gone courting in the village. Even though an elderly gentleman — eleven and a bit — he was still keenly interested in ladies, and at first nobody worried much.

When night fell, and he still had not come back, anxiety began to mount. Six months earlier he had gone off rabbiting and become wedged down a burrow, from which, after widespread searches, he had had to be exhumed. On that occasion he had stayed out overnight, but next day someone had heard him barking underground, and he was safely home in less than twenty-four hours.

Now it seemed likely that he had gone to ground again. On Saturday morning friends staying for the weekend, ourselves among them, were despatched to investigate various fox earths and badger setts in the neighbourhood, but we found no signs of recent digging, and heard no faint barks answering our calls.

Sal felt instinctively that the old boy was somewhere close at hand — and all day I found myself thinking of another incident in which a black retriever had vanished, out in the country, in the middle of the day. Then, too, the owner had persistently sensed that the bitch was not far away, and when the mystery was solved — the dog was found two days later, alive and in good order, at the bottom of an ancient, dry well into which she had fallen — the intuition proved to have been perfectly correct.

But there was no quick end to *our* search. On Sunday gloom deepened. Henry's companion Bodger, another fox terrier, was clearly missing his friend, even if he did enjoy the extra attention which he was getting. Among the humans, hope dwindled.

The worst thing was not knowing what had happened. Although it seemed most likely that Henry was stuck underground, he could also have been accidentally shut into some building, run over on the main road or even kidnapped. It was also possible that he had been killed by a badger whose sett he had invaded. Yet the strongest probability was simply that he had become wedged in a tunnel and that, as he grew weaker, he would starve to death.

Earlier I described the difficulties which we had at home when a farmer lost a new-born calf. That animal stood two feet at the shoulder, weighed a hundred pounds, and was above ground. Even so, we searched for more than forty-eight hours before we found it. Henry, about six inches at the shoulder and out of sight, offered an infinitely more difficult target — not exactly a needle in a haystack, but a small and elderly victim of his own impetuosity, prematurely buried in one of the numerous earthworks dotted about the wolds.

Departing guests left the household in a state of dejection, which deepened as the week progressed. For day after day Sal spent hours exploring the local earths: she went, of course, to the place where Henry had been stuck before, and she excavated several other likely burrows, assisted by Bodger, who occasionally raised her hopes by showing interest at the mouth of a particular hole; but as he was at least as keen on rabbits as on finding Henry, his assistance was of questionable value, and yielded no result.

When hard frost set in, and the temperature stayed below freezing for three days on end, Sal almost gave up. In desperation, she invoked local members of the RSPCA who had located another dog by means of some home-made stethoscope. This, it turned out, was not available, so they came instead with the flexible tube of a vacuum-cleaner, which they stuck down earth after earth, alternately calling and listening.

By the second weekend, hope was all-but dead. On the morning of Monday — the tenth day — Sal went off exercising her horse, and Richard, her husband, was preparing to go into Bridlington to put an offer of reward in the local newspaper — something which he had meant but failed to do the week before. He was also planning to call on a stone-mason and commission a small round plaque, incised with Henry's details and the legend *Cave Cerbere* — 'Watch out, Cerberus' — warning the great hound which in classical mythology guards the entrance to the underworld that a snappy little recruit was on his way down.

Then, sitting in his study, he heard a commotion. Peter, who helps with the horses and in the house, had gone to the door, and there, lying on the step, was a dishevelled and utterly exhausted fox terrier. Though extremely weak, and a great deal thinner than when last seen, he was still able to put over the message that he wished to be conveyed to the Aga as soon as possible.

The fact that his coat was packed with sand suggested that, having shrunk physically, he had at last managed to force himself backwards out of the tunnel in which he had been trapped. Furthermore, the texture of the sand indicated that he had indeed been very close at hand, as Sal had thought.

Richard's problem now was to break the good news gently. He put a bottle of champagne on ice, but he knew that if he called to Sal as she came back from her ride, she would leap off the horse and run into the house, and the odds were that the horse would take off too. To avoid an accident, he arranged that when Peter saw her coming he would intercept her, say there was someone on the telephone, and take the horse back to the stable while she went in. So in she went — to be confronted by a miracle.

After a highly-charged reunion, Henry was found to be in amazingly good order. A vet pronounced him none the worse: his insides were functioning, and on a diet of warm milk and baby food he quickly began to recover. Although it was possible that he had killed and eaten a rabbit, it was certain — since all surface water had turned to ice — that he could not have drunk anything for ten days.

The question now is whether or not he has learnt his lesson. Since his return he has been under close supervision, but he has a great knack of slipping away when nobody is looking, and everyone concerned fervently hopes that he will not wreck Christmas by means of another disappearing act. Little does he know that his mistress is researching to see if there is any form of pinger, or transponder, which could be fixed to his collar or implanted in some part of his anatomy, so that if he does go to ground again, it will be possible to locate him, like a ferret, electronically.

Meanwhile, he has received letters and postcards of congratulation — and well he may, for his was surely an outstanding feat of survival. What fascinates me is the question of his physical and mental state during the 240-odd hours of his incarceration.

What was he doing all that time? Was he able to move at all? Could he turn round, or was he completely stuck? And what was he thinking?

I do not believe that animals have any conception of death. Henry cannot therefore have been frightened of dying. But he must have suffered greatly from hunger and thirst; and all the time, as his strength declined, there must have flickered in his brain some idea of the place he loved — the house, the kitchen, his bean-bag by the Aga — some dim but potent recollection which eventually drew him home.

Powers of the Fox

It began on a morning of bright moonlight about half an hour before dawn. As I awoke I heard a curious noise which I could not immediately identify: neither a croon nor a moan nor yet a hum, it seemed to be emanating from the farmyard below our bedroom window.

With my head in the open, I heard it more clearly, from half-left. It was a cat, advising some other creature, probably feline, to get lost. But then from my right came another sound — a hard-edged, high-pitched mixture of rattle, scrape and jitter, a scratter or jittle, almost mechanical in its harshness.

Magpies, I thought — for magpies do make quasi-mechanical noises when squabbling on their roost. But as I hung out of the window, watching and listening, the long, dark shape of a fox slipped up over the garden wall and stood on the lawn beneath me. When I clicked my fingers, it fled over the grass, silent as a ghost. Moments later, a cat descended from its safe perch on the straw bales in the barn and stalked away, tail erect, towards the lane.

At least the moaning noise was explained: the cat had been cursing the fox. But what had made that peculiar rattle? It might not have been the fox at all; but because the animal appeared from the same direction as the noise, I naturally connected the two: it was as if the fox had been trying to dig its way into one of the outbuildings, scrabbling at the door.

Over the next few nights that elusive sound began to haunt us. My wife heard it early one morning, away to the left as she looked out over the yard, and she thought a fox was trying to break into the barn which houses the chickens. That same evening she heard it once more, this time at the kitchen door.

As we went to bed it came yet again, from the farmyard. By then I had a torch to hand, but the source of the noise was beyond a birch tree which stands on the lawn, and the beam broke up in its branches.

Although not scared, we were certainly puzzled, and spent some time speculating about the identity of our mysterious visitor. We assumed it was the fox which I had seen on the lawn; but it could also have been a badger. I started to wonder if it had one of its feet caught in a trap or snare, which it was dragging: metal or wire would make that kind of noise. Yet the fox which came over the wall had certainly not been burdened by any encumbrance.

Two mornings later a lame fox appeared in the paddock above the garden, carrying one front paw. Was this our nocturnal prowler, now free of its impediment? Whatever had happened to its foot, the injury was by no means incapacitating, for that evening we saw it catch and kill a rook. Next day, as I let the dogs out, there were *two* foxes wrangling or mating (or both) on the same spot.

None of this caused us much concern, for even if we were surrounded by foxes every night, they could not reach our chickens, and were doing us no harm. But then another element entered the story.

A few miles away in the hills, the death occurred of a well-known landowner and country sportsman. Although I had never met him, I did know some of his family and friends, and soon I was hearing how, on their way by car to his interment, several of them had been astonished to see a fox sitting by the road at the end of the dead man's drive. It had killed a rat, and was making a leisurely meal.

Not only did the animal hold its ground when the mourners slowed down: an hour later, when they drove back from the church, it was still there, in the middle of the day. What all of them remembered most clearly was the way it stared coolly at them with its amber eyes.

The incident let loose a flood of reminiscence in the neighbourhood. As it happened, the dead man had never been a great chaser of foxes; but stories of foxes appearing mysteriously during the funerals of hunting men, or hanging about outside their houses after death, are by no means uncommon.

Most of them, it is true, concern other parts of the country, are set in the past, and are no more than hearsay. A typical anecdote, told by a friend in the village, relates how a famous hunting man died, and a friend of his, who knew perfectly well that he should go to the funeral, allowed himself to be seduced to Scotland by the offer of a week's fishing. Scarcely had he made his first cast into the river when he looked up and saw, sitting on the far bank, an old grey fox which glared at him so balefully that he could not fish any more.

Several weird tales were collected by the Countess of Feversham in *Strange Stories of the Chase,* published twenty years ago. In that little anthology one can read how, to the Gormanston family of Co. Meath, foxes have for centuries been associated with death, and how, in October 1907, a pack of them came by night to besiege the chapel in which Colonel the Hon. Richard Preston was keeping watch over the body of his father, the 14th Viscount, recently deceased. When Preston opened the door, and candlelight fell on the assembled horde, he was 'very conscious of the golden-yellow stare'.

Although I do not doubt the authenticity of such stories, they happened (as I say) far away. But then we had this incident close to home, witnessed by our own down-to-earth country people. Furthermore, it was by no means the first of its kind.

Locals talk freely about the astonishing hunt which took place after the death of Major Gerald Gundry, the celebrated Joint Master of the Duke of Beaufort's hounds, whose kennels are just down the road at Badminton. Scarcely had he been buried, last winter, when the hounds, after meeting miles away, took an unprecedented line, ran the whole way back to his home at Shipton Moyne and killed a fox outside his front door.

Even creepier was the experience of the tenth Duke of Beaufort, known to friends and colleagues as Master, and one of the most formidable hunting men of all time. Early one Sunday morning in 1984, when he was eighty-five, he went out for his usual walk before breakfast accompanied by his fox terrier Ajax, and there in the churchyard at Badminton he saw three foxes, one sitting on his grandfather's grave, one on his father's, and the third in the open.

Such a blithe old fellow was Master that he found nothing sinister in this: on the contrary, he was delighted that Ajax had a great hunt scattering the intruders. But to Daphne Moore, a friend in Badminton village to whom he reported the phenomenon, the triple visitation could have only one meaning. 'The third fox was for him, of course,' she says, 'and sure enough, he died the following Sunday'.

None of this, I know, has any direct connection with the scrabbling noise in our farmyard. But on Christmas morning yet another fox stood on the frosty meadow above the house and gazed down for several minutes with what could have been interest or contempt. Through binoculars, I could pick out the steady glow of its amber eyes.

Once you start half-believing that foxes have some supernatural power which enables them to detect when humans are about to expire, or have recently done so — especially humans who have persecuted their kind — you find it hard to put the notion out of your mind, particularly at this time of year, when the nights are long and dark, and the year itself is dying.